The Da
For

A Daily Dose of Inspiration for Every Day of the Year

By Kacey Coppola Morreale

Additional Inspiration by Kate Coppola Leiva
& Kara Coppola Schmahl

Ordering Information:
Orders by U.S. trade bookstores and wholesalers.
Please visit CreateSpace.com

Published in the United States of America
ISBN-13: 978-1544629544
ISBN-10: 1544629540

First Edition

The Daily Soul Sessions and its materials are not intended to treat, diagnose, cure, or prevent any pregnancy or non-pregnancy related issues. All material in The Daily Soul Sessions is provided for inspirational purposes only. Always seek the advice of your physician or other qualified health care provider with any questions you have regarding a medical condition, and before undertaking any diet, exercise, or other health program.

Books in The Daily Soul Sessions Series:

The Daily Soul Sessions For The Pregnant Mama
The Daily Soul Sessions For Every Mama

Available on Amazon now.

Want more inspiration?
Go to *TheDailySoulSessions.com* to get your
30 Day Journaling Challenge!
Each day has a new journal prompt that encourages you to dig deep
and open up your creative well. No prompt takes longer than 10
minutes if you don't want it to, so there are no excuses!

Get Your Free Lullaby Download by Leaving a Review on Amazon!
Please help spread the word and the love by leaving a review on
Amazon for The Daily Soul Sessions For Every Mama

After you leave a review, send a screenshot of your review to
contact@thedailysoulsessions.com and we will send you a free
download of the soothing lullaby "*Light*" by Kate and Kacey
Coppola! Sweetly rock those babes to sleep...zzzzzz.

Praise for
The Daily Soul Sessions For The Pregnant Mama

Pregnant, or know someone who is?
Check out what other moms-to-be are saying about
The Daily Soul Sessions for the Pregnant Mama book…
280 inspirations, one for every day of pregnancy!

"The Daily Soul Sessions is a special project that helps comfort and celebrate mothers-to-be with spiritual depth. I wish I had stopped googling all my symptoms during my pregnancy and instead enjoyed the weird and wonderful miracle; this book helps pregnant women do just that. I can't think of a better gift to a soon-to-be mother than to help her cherish herself at the start of this very special journey."

~Rachel Jansen, mama to Genevieve
Account Manager, British Vogue

"There is a lot of material out there for pregnant women but not much that simply acknowledges the changes, challenges and little miracles we experience daily without giving advice and listing all the "what not to do's". Reading The Daily Soul Sessions was like sitting with that friend who makes you laugh and says the right thing when you need to hear it."

~Ann Williams, mama to Brennan and Regan
Jeweler (Evermoreco.com)

"This is the perfect book for any mom-to-be. During pregnancy so many women get wrapped up in all things baby; what to expect when the baby arrives and how to take care of the baby, that they often lose sight of their own needs. In just a short passage each day, The Daily Soul Sessions reminds us to take a minute for ourselves to become the best possible woman and mama that we can be."

~Kate LaMaster Mruczkowski, mama to Carter and Grant
Creative Manager at Curb Music Publishing

Praise for
The Daily Soul Sessions For Every Mama

Take the next step in your mothering journey with
The Daily Soul Sessions For Every Mama book...
365 inspirations, one for every day of the year!

"From the first page, I was inspired and uplifted to be the best mama and WOMAN I can be. Each page I felt like they were speaking directly to my mama heart; my inner soul. The interactive and reflective manner draws you in making it easy to engage and embrace the individuality of yourself while continuously celebrating the union and bond of motherhood. It is intuitive and inspirational; a daily dose of self love, personal reflection and authentic passion for humankind. Get ready to change your life and your daily soul."

~Amanda Maxwell, mama to Declan
Blogger at PishtoPosh.com

"Motherhood is a journey unlike anything else. We are asked to trust that doing our best is enough. To trust that no matter how big the struggle feels, that it too shall pass. We are asked to embrace the moment. To see the world through the eyes of our children. It's a big job! It's challenging and can feel like it's never ending; yet it's the most rewarding job I've personally ever had. But as all of us mamas out there know, some days you just need a serious pick me up! You need a jolt of inspiration to get you through your day. This book is just that. Filled with love and laughter and truth about what it really means to be a mother. This book is a breath of fresh air. A simple, yet profound read, that I actually have time to enjoy every day!"

~Chelsea Rothert, mama to Matteo
DONA certified Birth Doula, Childbirth Educator and Prenatal
Yoga Teacher (Empowered-Pregnancy.com)

This book is for our babies…Kaylie, Billy, and Sylvie.

You guys solidified this whole mamahood thing, and we couldn't be more grateful for you.

This book is also for all you precious mothers out there on the same path as we are. To creativity. To inspiration. To happiness. To love.

Introduction

We have been songwriters for the past 17 years. The art of writing a song is in the three minutes it takes to tell a story, to change the life of the person listening in some small way. We write about life; its struggles, its miracles, its magic. And over time, those three-minute songs became meditations, became prayers...became this book.

Becoming a mom changed my life, rocked my world, stressed me out—you name it, I've felt it. And yes, becoming a mom is magical, but it is also the hardest thing I have ever done.

How is one supposed to navigate this uncharted territory? The tantrums and tickles, messes and kisses—the constant push and pull of striving to hang on to who I used to be and embracing the person I am now. Well, a glass of wine always helps...but so does this book.

Let's get real. Happiness doesn't just happen. There is no quick fix. There is no secret that once discovered will make you happy for the rest of your life. It takes effort. It takes consistency. It takes faith. The small choices we make every single day lead to a great relationship, a fulfilling job, or a healthy lifestyle. And all of those components add up to happiness. These motherhood years are incredible and impossible all at the same time. So how do we maximize our memories and just be happy amidst the dirty diapers, the dirty laundry, and the dirty hair? Yeah you heard me—dry shampoo is a game changer, but it can only get us so far!

So let's get real. This book is *your* journal. Read it over and over. It's your daily pick me up every morning to get your mind right and find the inspiration in motherhood. It's your friendly reminder to choose love every time—*especially* when you don't think you can. When we make the choice to be mindful and show our kids the magic in the small things, our hearts will blossom right along with theirs. And you will have found your happiness, Mama. Are you with me? It's gonna take commitment—but we already know all about that.

And let's get real. A happy mama can change the world.

January

New Beginnings

The Daily Soul Sessions For Every Mama

January 1

"I still find each day too short for all the thoughts I want to think, all the walks I want to take, all the books I want to read, and all the friends I want to see."
~John Burroughs, Writer & Naturalist

Boredom is not an option. Erase that word from your vocabulary. This year—make that bucket list—and check those dreams off. Don't narrow it down to only grandiose things that will take time and money. Those are dreams you should absolutely work toward, but what could be on that list that you could do today?

Fall madly in love with your life, and happiness will follow. Your marriage to yourself is much like a marriage to a spouse. Time, effort, magic, spontaneity all has to be worked on. There are so many dishes to be tasted, stories to be told, sunrises to be seen. It's a brand new year...and that's not boring at all.

January 2

"She loves the smell of coffees, bloomed roses, and new beginnings." ~Sonia Azalia

Ahhhhh. New beginnings. Ya gotta love new beginnings. The mornings that I wake up ready and willing to be seduced by the day are always the best ones. Thank goodness for sunrises—they give you a blank slate every day. A chance to do something you've never done before, start something you were too scared to start yesterday, be someone you have always wanted to be. New beginnings come in all shapes and sizes. We just have to be open enough to try them out when they cross our path.

So take a deep breath—*right now*—wherever you are, and find some new beginning in your life. *"She loved the smell of new beginnings..."*. Of hope, of relief, of adventure...of peace.

January 3

The flower for the month of January is the carnation. Kind of dull, right? Not so fast, Mama, because the carnation represents deep love and fascination. I absolutely adore this. Don't we all want to start this bold and bright new year with endless amounts of fascination? Fascination for yourself, your kids, your husband—and all the delicious dreams and adventures this year is about to bring. Find ways to fall in love with your new year. The possibilities are endless...so which one fascinates you?

Dream Lives Journal Exercise
Spend 15 minutes and write down your five dream lives (Courtesy of The Artist's Way, by Julia Cameron). If you could be anything in the world, what would you be? Think outside the box, think big, be bold. Don't let your "reality" or the "why nots" get in the way. This is what you would be regardless of caretaker, mother, or any other label you've already put on yourself. You will be so inspired by the dreams inside you that are dying to come out this year.

January 4

Those mornings I wake up before the alarm clock, the baby, or the street sweeper—I secretly love them. There is a sweet spot in dawn where magic happens. Even on a winter morning, the energy will invigorate you, I promise. Listen to the quiet, enjoy a hot beverage, write in your journal. You may be surprised at what inspiration comes your way. Get your soul centered so you can share yourself with the rest of your world. The noise will come running soon enough.

"The breeze at dawn has secrets to tell you. Don't go back to sleep." ~Rumi

January 5

The New Year is filled with fresh ideas, reinvigorated dreams, and bursts of determination. That is why I love the new year. It is pure possibility bottled up like a lovely little Prosecco…and I am a sucker for both. Keep your mind open to the excitement this time of year inevitably brings.

January 6

Doubt is the devil, and within days of a new pursuit all the fears and "why nots" can creep in. We have to learn to ignore that side of ourselves and learn tricks that can change our mindset when the fear sneaks in. Who and what is your support system made up of? These are the people and things that bring you back to yourself and remind you *why* you want to achieve the things you dream of. For me it's my family, a persuading and motivating dream board, a loving husband, and two daughters I want to show how magical life can be. Go after this new year with passion. You can do it. *Whatever you want.* You can be the person you truly want to be. We are all a work in progress, and I learn new things every single day. Looking back on last New Years, I am stopped in my tracks at what happened this past year. Things I went after and totally surprising things that weren't even on my radar, both of which came to fruition.

It's life. We just have to have the courage to live it.

January 7

"You know all those things you've always wanted to do? You should go do them."
~E.J. Lamprey, Author

Let's stop wishing, stop waiting, and start doing. The point is not the endgame, it's the journey. We've heard all that before of course, but I still find myself thinking...*I'll really be happy when*...when what? You lose that baby weight? You get that promotion? This year I'm not going to wait around.

There's just not enough time—and my real life begins now.

January 8

Take one moment before the day begins and think back on your life. Right now. Name five obstacles, milestones, battles that you have won. Heck, having a baby is a big one right there! Feel the triumph that comes from knowing you can survive anything...because you have. You're not dead yet. Remember the person you were—look at the person you are. Imagine the person you will be. Then go be her.

January 9

"She feels in Italics and thinks in Capitals." ~Henry James

I. Love. This. Quote. I read an opinion that if you write in capitals you are essentially yelling at whomever you are speaking to. I couldn't disagree more—and that person is most likely not Italian. Or Irish. Or a woman. Or…passionate. Free spirits speak with their hands, find true excitement in the small things, and love pumpkin spice lattes. And they smile. A lot. This age is not a time for meekness. It is not a time for coloring inside the lines. It is a time for invention, inspiration, and love.

I feel inspired today. DO YOU?!

January 10

The element this month is AIR. Fitting, isn't it? All the resolution and hope that a new year rings in, swirls and floats around us in the cold January air. We just have to be open to reaching out and grasping them as they move by.

Breathe deeply, until sweet air extinguishes the burn of fear in your lungs and every breath is a beautiful refusal to become anything less than infinite."
~D. Antoinette Foy, Writer

We are the teachers and the dream followers for our children. They will never learn to fly unless we first show them how. If that isn't a reason to go after what you want, what is?

January 11

Visualize: form a mental image of; imagine. (Google.com)

How can you cultivate a visualization practice in your life this year? To visualize something—a goal, a dream, a hope for the future—is to make it real in your mind. You think of whatever it is that you want, and suddenly a picture enters your head. Like magic, something that didn't exist all of a sudden enters your reality. The key now is to take that mental image one step further. You have to *really feel* the emotions that come into your body when you think about your dream. Think about it as if it has already come true, as if it already exists in your world. That bubbling feeling of excitement, of joy, of satisfaction? Train yourself to actually feel those emotions in every cell of your being. See yourself in your mind's eye already having what it is you wish for.

Food for thought: Scientists at Harvard are actually proving that thinking about playing the piano and actually playing the piano produce the same positive changes in our brains (http://content.time.com/time/magazine/article/0,9171,1580438,00.html). So visualize. Everyday. Make your dreams come true.

January 12

The new year comes with hope and anticipation. The new year also comes with the heaviness of the unknown. Don't let the weight get to you today. Go into this day with joy and optimism. Encourage everyone you see with that mindset. That is all life is—a mindset. Decide it is so…and so it shall be. It's contagious.

"Today I shall behave as if this is the day I shall be remembered." ~Dr. Seuss

January 13

Have you begun to practice a morning ritual? It is so invigorating to carve out time for ourselves before the chaos of the kids and the day take over. Try this five step morning ritual this week. It will absolutely start your day out in an inspiring and positive way.

MORNING RITUAL:
1.) Get up 30 minutes earlier than normal.
2.) Breathe consciously by inhaling and exhaling slowly for at least seven cycles. Then meditate, pray, or say some positive affirmations.
3.) Finish a large glass of water.
4.) Read your Daily Soul Session.
5.) Do one of the following:
~Write in your journal
~Do a quick morning yoga or stretch session (longer if you can!)
~Read a couple of pages from an inspirational book

Prepare to have an amazing day!

January 14

Choose love, choose love, choose love. How can two simple words possibly be so powerful? If you let them, they have the power to completely transform your life. When your toddler wakes up way too early—choose love over annoyance. When your husband doesn't remember to tell you you're out of coffee—choose love over frustration. When you're worried about an upcoming deadline or family member or bills to be paid—choose love over fear. It sounds easy, but it is a constant choice we have to make. Try it today. Try it again tomorrow. And keep choosing love for each day thereafter. It's as simple as saying "I choose love" when faced with an obstacle. *I choose love.*

January 15

This path we are on—can anyone really understand it but you? Your hopes, your dreams, your vision for your life. Can anyone really make those things your reality but you? We often find ourselves making excuses: *oh if only I had more time to myself or more help with the kids, then maybe I could get all of the things done that I need to.* This is a slippery slope to fall down. No excuses. Live in the present, Mama...and then make darn sure you make the absolute best you can out of it.

"It's your road. And yours alone. Others may walk it with you, but no one can walk it for you." ~Rumi

January 16

Let's take this year one day at a time. A new year is just that. New. It's an open road, but we do not have to have the road map for 365 days drawn out today. Set attainable daily goals for yourself and forget the rest in the moment. Don't get lost in the bigger picture— that can cause stress, doubt, negativity. Do the work and the dreaming for today. And then start again tomorrow.

"Anxiety happens when you think you have to figure out everything all at once. Breathe. You're strong. You got this. Take it day by day." ~Karen Salmansohn, Author

January 17

The mornings when I actually wake up early enough to write in my journal are always—*always*—the best ones. Before the kids wake up, while I drink my coffee...sometimes I just write down words I love. Whimsy. Magic. Light. Love. All these words are so lovely. I want to swallow them whole. Dancing, candlelight, gardens, fairies, mystery. How can I gather more of the energy of these words, these ideas, into my life? Just do it, right? Just believe it. It is hard to find time for all of these "things" I want to be right now. I suppose I should just wake up earlier. Well sure, that's a given! But even so...nature walks, trees, flowers, sunlight, ocean, sparkle, shimmer...

It's truly amazing to just open your eyes and breathe in the light. Feel it fuel you, fire you, light your soul from the inside. Be the person you yearn to be. Maybe this year we can just believe. Just like that. Just believe because we can. We all have that power within us—and today is a perfect day to start believing. Today is the perfect day to be fully present and fully you.

January 18

"I didn't always know what I wanted to do, but I knew the kind of woman I wanted to be." ~Diane von Furstenberg

You don't have to have it all figured out all the time. Give yourself room to breathe and time to get to know yourself and your desires. If this New Year is giving you pause and leaving you a little lost as to next steps, it's ok. Deep down you already know what kind of woman you want to be. Just come back to that—those characteristics you want to show your family and the world. The actions will come from that. They always do.

January 19

Trying new things is so challenging. And so invigorating. It's what makes a new romance seductive, a new talent satisfying. It banishes routine and forces you to live in the moment. And the best part? It can be something as big as jumping out of an airplane or as small as learning to make the perfect espresso. These triumphs we gather along the way are what make us who we are, and they give us our unique story that we get to share with the people we meet. What can you do this week that you have never done before? Find that life force and go experience it.

January 20

Sometimes the hardest step is the very first one. Just like with a baby, that first shaky step toward a new goal is so filled with the unknown, it can almost paralyze you from taking it. The 'what ifs' are still possible, and the dream hasn't succeeded or failed yet. But the fear is there. The fear that this new dream is not going to work out, the fear that your past will catch up to you, the fear that you won't know how to see this new goal through.

Enough. Today, this year…enough fear. The time for taking that first step has come.

"As I walked out the door to the gate that would lead to my freedom, I knew if I didn't leave my bitterness and hatred behind, I'd still be in prison." ~Nelson Mandela

January 21

Today is National Hugging Day!

"Hugs were invented to let people know you love them without having to say anything." ~Unknown

Are you a hugger? I'm a hugger. I hug my friends and family, and I hug people I've just met. It's just easier to lead with a hug than lead with an awkward...handshake? Nod? Wave? Today, be a hugger! Just try it and feel the warmth of human connection spread through you. Hug your dog, hug your neighbor, hug your kids (even when they resist!), hug someone you're just introduced to. And give yourself a hug while you're at it. Right now, close your eyes and wrap both arms around your body and squeeze tight. Continue that hold for three deep breaths—in and out, in and out, in and out. Then release your arms and feel the energy pulsing through them, from your shoulders to the tips of your fingers. Take another deep breath and raise your arms out to the sides and above your head. Interlace your fingers and press your arms up to the sky and exhale. Really stretch as you inhale again. Exhale as you bring both arms down, stretching out to the sides as you do. Open your eyes. Now go hug the first person or animal you see. Share that gorgeous, vibrant, positive, loving energy!

January 22

Why not? Why not, Mama? Why not you? Why not this year? Why not this dream? Why not that class? Why not that goal? Why not that house, that trip, that book, that opportunity? Why not...

"We come to recognize that God is unlimited in supply and that everyone has equal access." ~Julia Cameron, The Artist's Way

January 23

In honor of National Handwriting Day (yes, you heard me), I challenge all of us to sit down and write a handwritten note to someone we haven't talked to in a while. Someone that has had a positive effect on your life, someone that might not even know of the effect he or she had. Write to them, and say, "Hello, Happy New Year!" Thank them for being the inspiring, creative light in your life that they are. Let's give back to the world...one handwritten letter at a time.

January 24

"We are all broken, that's how the light gets in." ~Ernest Hemingway

New beginnings can bring painful memories with them. Anytime we want to embark on a new goal, follow a new passion, or start a new business—our old failures or negative outcomes always come creeping in. Starting right now, we need to totally switch our viewpoint on those obstacles. Turn your failures into wisdom, your negative outcomes into courage and determination. No one successful has ever gotten to where they are without experiencing failure on a fairly regular basis. But it's the fight in them, the willingness to get back up and keep going that makes them a success. That makes them inspirational. And that is what we need to chase after this year, Mama. Let the light in...don't fear your brokenness. It makes you strong, feisty—a warrior. It makes you a mother.

January 25

I think I can, I think I can, I think I can. Are you on the precipice of a decision today? Right on the edge of some huge leap of faith? There are so many quotes and sayings that can give you courage to just say yes. That even if you shoot and miss the moon, you'll land among the stars. And really, what's the worst that can happen? But honestly there is one quote that can suffuse your heart, body, and soul with determination and courage today...

"God is within her, she will not fall." ~Psalm 46:5

So go fly today, Mama.

January 26

"Tension is who you think you should be.
Relaxation is who you are."
~Chinese Proverb

As you continue to shape your year ahead and get into the swing of new habits and dreams, it can stress you out at times, right? I want to find the balance between pushing myself and accepting myself. We all want to keep growing and changing our destinies for the better. We all want to achieve goals, be successful, and enjoy life more. We all want to be the best moms and wives and women we can be. But we have to love ourselves first. We cannot be constantly riding the tension of who we aren't yet...we need to find some awesome sauce in who we already are. So celebrate that today, Mama. Who you are. The complicated, sexy, confident, sparkling soul that you already are.

January 27

Fear is a powerful motivator. A motivator to do nothing. To remain in the same rut. The only thing that conquers fear is faith. That's all we have when we decide to put one foot in front of the other over and over again. Striving after new goals within your family and yourself is as exciting as it is challenging. And fear can be a constant companion if we don't learn to fight back. With gratitude, faith, and positive affirmations of what we know is true and good and inspiring.

"I want to be a woman who overcomes obstacles by tackling them in faith instead of tiptoeing around them in fear." ~Renee Swope

January 28

You discover what you are made of when you become a mother. Maybe you haven't always dreamed of having a family. Maybe it was just a given in the back of your mind, but you've always been much more career focused. Becoming a mom forces us to open our world in a way we could never have dreamed possible. Yes, by having this wonderful miracle in the form of a child placed in our care…but also by opening our minds, hearts, and souls to WHO WE REALLY ARE—because motherhood can completely take over your life if you let it. It can swallow you whole until you barely recognize the woman you were before.

Motherhood teaches us how to fight to *hold onto us*. It teaches us how to continue to follow our dreams so we can in turn show our kids what life is all about: truly being brave enough to live a life devoted to sharing and spreading love and light. Motherhood continues to teach us how to be the living, breathing example of that devotion every single day. Motherhood allows us to become the fierce and inspiring woman we all want to be.

January 29

"And now that you don't have to be perfect, you can be good." ~John
Steinbeck, <u>East of Eden</u>

Roll up your sleeves, and get to work this year. Feel the weight that
striving for perfection takes on your shoulders...and don't be afraid to
toss it off a cliff as soon as possible. There is freedom in not taking
ourselves so very seriously. Freedom to create. Freedom to try new
things. Freedom to laugh at ourselves. Freedom to live.

January 30

Good morning, beautiful soul. It is a brand new dawn—and this sun
has never risen over this day before. So make these 24 hours count.
Have you bought a new journal for this year yet? The first step to
leaping into your dreams (and out of a rut!) is by journaling. When
you give voice and shape to your inner desires—good and bad—you
can weed through them, and take the first action toward living the
life you long for.

January 31

January is almost over, but this year has just begun. It can be a scary time—this cavern of the unknown. Why not spin that abyss around, and see it as a chasm of potential. Of *what ifs*. Of *if you start today, imagine where you shall be one year from now*. We do not know the twists and turns that are ahead of us this year. But the possibilities are heady and intoxicating. And fun. Start with a positive attitude—start with yes—and the inspiration will follow.

"I know nothing of any certainty, but the sight of the stars makes me dream."
~Vincent van Gogh

FEBRUARY

Love

February 1

The second month of this year is upon us. The element of February is *FIRE*. It is a month for stoking the fire within you—for continuing this journey of what lights your inner pilot light, what feeds your soul and passions. Being an inspired, dream following woman will make us much more inspiring mamas. This is what I tell myself every time the trials and routine of motherhood wear on me. Every time I feel the lack of time creep in. Every time I need a kick in the pants to not let life just pass me by as I cling to sanity and sleep deprivation. Light that fire today. Let's get it burning to a brilliant flame, so the intriguing and fascinating woman you are can be seen for miles and miles.

February 2

Love. Tis the month of love. Love for your mate, for your children, for your friends. And most especially—love for yourself. Yes, I am looking straight at you, Mama. Self love is the start of all love. If you can't love yourself, you will never be able to truly love others. That is what I want to pass on to my children almost more than anything else. How to truly love. Love the world they are blessed to live in, love their friends and family with passions deep, someday love a spouse with generosity and respect, and love themselves—for the fascinating souls they are.

"The more you extend kindness to yourself the more it will become your automatic response to others." ~Wayne Dyer, Philosopher, Author

February 3

Invite confidence in this month, Mama. Be steadfast in your morning affirmation, intention setting, and prayer. Like attracts like—if we can find a way to tap into our inner confidence, then our job as mothers and women is halfway done. Confidence is so powerful and beautiful; don't you just want to infuse your kids with it? The first step is to lead by example. Show them the confidence to try new things. To follow a dream. To lead from out front. To say no. To say yes. To love. To be themselves.

Confidence: *A feeling of self-assurance arising from one's appreciation of one's own abilities or qualities. The feeling or belief that one can rely on someone or something; firm trust. (Google.com)*

February 4

"Doubt kills more dreams than failure ever will." ~Suzy Kassem, Writer, Poet

Refuse the doubt today. Refuse the doubt when it tries to creep in and paint a veil of fear in whatever dream or task you've set for yourself. Push through to the other side. A successful woman is only successful because she just keeps trying. So don't ever give up or give in. There is light and relief and vindication waiting.

February 5

Are you in love with your life, Mama? Like head over heels, first date, butterflies, and giddy in love with your life? The key to happiness is to find that feeling of falling in love over and over again as much as we can. With our spouses, with our kids, with our jobs, with ourselves. To not be so self-sacrificing in life that we forget to make a little time for the things that get your heart racing. The things you think maybe you shouldn't take the time for or spend the money on, the class you are a little scared but a lot excited to sign up for. Fall in love with your life...by filling it with the things and people and experiences that you love.

What are five things you love that you could get involved with this month? Classes, hobbies, a workout, coffee with a friend, a book club, a hike, a date night...sign up and feel that joy take over.

February 6

Let's start this day out with a journal session. Or an art session. Finish the phrases with honesty or humor...but most of all love...

I love my hair today because...
I love my skin today because...
I love my husband today because...
I love breakfast time because...
I love doing dishes because...
I love the month of February because...
I love winter because...
I love taking care of my children because...
I love my house because...
I love my goals because...

Learn to love every single aching, reeling, frustrating, surprising, fabulous moment.

February 7

Sometimes we just need to stop. And take a big old deep breath. We tell our children to calm down all the time. Deep breaths, deep breaths, right? Come back to yourself. Your core. We aren't supposed to have this whole parent thing perfectly figured out. We learn, our children learn...and we grow. So take heart, Mama. You are figuring this out as you go. And that is exactly how it was designed to be.

"Experience: the most brutal of teachers. But you learn. My God, do you learn."
~C.S. Lewis

February 8

"Don't try to change life, but change the way you look at it. Make peace with this moment, be kind and be gentle to yourself." ~Ajahn Brahm, Buddhist Monk

Self love. Keep practicing self love this whole month long, Mama. Learn to love yourself for all your flaws, all your fears, all your insecurities. Then you can love your husband in the same way. Then you can teach your children to love others that way too.

February 9

We will never be as old or as young as we are in this moment. The wisdom you carry and the lessons to come strike a delicately awesome balance within. Respect that balance. Encourage the confidence that wisdom in womanhood brings, but stay open to the idea that we still have a lot to learn. A lot. And love every delicious scent, taste, feel, sound, and sight that we are blessed with today. Because as we know—life is both short and long—and it's all about staying in the moment.

February 10

"I laugh at myself. I don't take myself completely seriously. I think that's another quality that people have to hold on to…you have to laugh, especially at yourself."
~Madonna

Laughter can equal love sometimes. If you can find the humor in any situation, you are steps and steps above most people. They say it's the best medicine, and it's true—a good belly massaging laugh brings people together and binds them in happiness. Let's try to bring out the funny in ourselves, our partners, and our children today. Be goofy. Be silly. Be authentic. That is what your children want from you. Not the perfect, no hair out of place mama—but the real one. So they know that their silliness and quirks and authenticity are the most beautiful things about them too.

February 11

Love the Senses Journal Exercise
Love is the most powerful emotion in our existence. When we are receptive and open to the infinite amount of love around us, fear and negativity cannot exist. Take a few moments today to work on opening yourself up to the love in your life. Finish the following prompt, and get creative with it. What is in your immediate aura that you can be thankful for...and fall in love with all over again.

I love the sight of...
I love the sound of...
I love the taste of...
I love the smell of...
I love the feel of...

February 12

How do we decide what makes us truly, soul deep, passion-filled happy? What drives our self love? As women and mothers, our needs and true loves can get buried under the needs of our families. We slowly conform and reshape to be the caregivers and comforters for everyone around us until we forget small parts of ourselves. The unique, inspirational, lovely parts that make us who we are. So where do we start this year in taking back our creativity? Where do we begin to find the small dazzling pieces of ourselves that make us unique?

"Document the moments you feel most in love with yourself—what you're wearing, who you're around, what you're doing. Recreate and repeat." ~Warsan Shire, Poet

February 13

"There is a fountain of youth: it is your mind, your talents, the creativity you bring to your life and the lives of people you love. When you learn to tap this force, you will truly have defeated age." ~Sophia Loren

This could be our mantra for the whole year. To learn to tap into our creativity in order to inspire everyone around us. To be that woman who people light up around. To cultivate passion and spontaneity and delight in the little things and the big things in life. Forever young and forever free.

February 14

Wife: *I love you.*
Husband: *I love you too.*
Wife: *Prove it. Scream it to the world.*
Husband: **whispers in her ear* I Love You.*
Wife: *Why'd you whisper it to me?*
Husband: *Because You are my World.*
~Unknown

February 15

Let's begin this day as we mean to go on. With purpose. No more stumbling to the coffee machine, bleary eyed and bitter—instead open yourself to the morning. Open yourself to the breath, to the crystal clear beauty of this brand new day. The birds are singing, they know how precious each day is. Imagine if the only way we communicated was through song. Every day would begin like that...With a song.

I had a song playing in my head today when I woke up. I reached over and turned on Pandora without thinking and that exact song started to play. Out of nowhere—or straight out of my head—the universe aligned. Profound moments like that fill me with spirit and awaken my senses to the magic that surrounds us every single day. Moments like that reaffirm my faith. Moments like that make me smile.

> *"And I've been trying to find*
> *What's been in my mind*
> *As the days keep turning into night."*
> ~Alexi Murdoch, "All of My Days"

Keep seeking. Keep searching...you'll find whatever it is you're looking for.

February 16

Soften your heart as you slowly awaken to the day. The love between you and your spouse grows to the most exquisite levels after you have kids. At the same time, quality time and intimacy gets harder and harder to manage. But that love still exists. And we have to stoke it and keep it burning as we manage all the chaos in our life. If you are still on your journey to finding that love, keep going. It's out there. One of the biggest blessings we can pass on to our kids is showing them what a healthy, loving, and respectful relationship looks like. It can be the most beautiful thing in the world...

"To intertwine your happiness with someone else's is so dangerously brave, so inherently idiotic, and so incomprehensibly, undeniably human." ~K Towne Jr., Poet

February 17

Self Love. What does that phrase mean to you? Does it mean not judging yourself? Forgiving yourself? Making time for yourself? Does it mean going to get a massage or a drink with friends? Perhaps it is thinking and speaking from a kind place when it comes to you. We would never say half the things to our friends and family that we say to ourselves. Self love starts from the very first minute we wake up and glance in a mirror. If I find an unflattering or negative thought forming, I try to immediately catch myself and mindfully replace that thought with its opposite. With something soothing, encouraging, and positive. Like a pebble in a lake, if we all practice self love today, the whole world will be a much better place.

February 18

Change is always around us. Some days change takes your breath away. And some days the subtleness of change blows in like a soft breeze—you look around, and it's been a month, a year, a lifetime. Birthdays, anniversaries, holidays smack us straight in the face with change. They are milestones you cannot ignore, and you cannot help but look back on the path that led you to where you are. But what about all the days in between? What about the random Thursday, your toddler running around like any other day, or your routine cup of coffee in hand as you take the elevator to work—what about that day? Stay mindful and grateful as much as you can, don't save those precious memories for only the big moments. Keep them flowing and constantly changing...keep them coming...

February 19

"The best way to predict the future is to create it." ~Abraham Lincoln

Our thoughts manifest our reality. If you have happy thoughts, you are most likely a happy person. If your thoughts lean toward worry and stress, then your days are typically filled with gloom and doom. Our thoughts are impressively powerful. Just taking a few extra minutes to mindfully empower your thoughts in the morning can completely change the direction of your day. Create the life you want right now—and then go live it. Exciting stuff, right?

February 20

Self Love Challenge Day! Choose something you absolutely love today, and make a plan to go do it. Hot stone massage? Book it. Getting lost in a library or bookstore for two hours? Call the babysitter, or tell the hubby he's on duty one evening. Wine tasting? Go to your local wine tasting spot and bring a friend—you don't have to fly to Napa. Make pottery, take a photography course, plant a flower, or have brunch at a swanky restaurant. We simply spend so much time taking care of our loved ones, we have to take care of ourselves every now and then. We have to refill our reserves of creativity and inspiration and self worth. You deserve to do something you love. But we have to actually book it—or it'll always be someday. Make it this day instead.

February 21

Go love the world today, Mama. Show our sons and daughters the power of positive actions and inspirational thought.

"Never do the jealousy, envy, and insecure stuff. Be the hustler, the well wisher, the go getter." ~Amy Howard, Social Media Strategist

February 22

Do you have a favorite number? Mine has always been 2. I like the balance of it, and I've always believed 2 is better than 1! Maybe that comes from being a twin. The number 2 just resonates with me, and it has always been my lucky number. So I'm inspired on this day…2/22…to live my life just knowing I've got luck on my side. I invite you to join me in the knowing. Even if 2 isn't your number, I'll lend it to you for the day. Walk through your morning, your afternoon, your evening feeling lucky, and I promise you—it will be a great day!

February 23

> *"Do what you feel in your heart is right: for you'll be criticized anyway."*
> ~Eleanor Roosevelt

"Hearts" are the theme for this month, so you might as well follow yours. In motherhood, friendship, and family. Follow your heart.

February 24

The end of a month can bring stagnancy and staleness. Especially in the darkness of winter. Can you feel spring yet? Most likely no, but try to find a little spring in your step somewhere today. Visit a flower shop and bring home some sunshine. Watch a beachy flick on TV or pinterest some vacation gems. Diffuse some geranium, lemon, and grapefruit essential oils. Sometimes the smallest of daily activities can invite in whatever it is that you are longing for.

February 25

Every day is a fresh start. A clean slate. A new beginning. Thank goodness. You can choose whatever path you want to take today. You can choose to lead your family, your children, and yourself in whatever direction inspires you. Because we lead by example. Today is the first day of the rest of your life...so how do you want to live it?

February 26

Procrastination: the act or habit of putting off or delaying, especially something requiring immediate attention. (Dictionary.com)

I find myself thinking about this word a lot lately. Not wanting to put things off that can be done right now, but unable to face another load of laundry or household chores. Heck, even changing another dirty diaper. Is it the stage of life we are in? Being a mom? Being a dad? Every moment of the day is focused outward on our families and on the life we are holding together. And in that chaos, you can forget about yourself. You can start to procrastinate on the dreams that still live inside your heart.

Take a minute today to sit quietly somewhere. Allow yourself a chance to remember the dreams that you've been too busy to think about. Is there one in there that still makes your heart beat faster? Is there something you can do right now to make one come true? Talk about being an inspiration to others. Make procrastination a thing of the past...and go after the future with delight today!

February 27

"Anyone can slay a dragon, he told me, but try waking up every morning and loving the world all over again. That's what takes a real hero." ~Brian Andreas, Storyteller

How about waking up every morning and parenting like it's the first day again and again. Not with fear or uncertainty, but with the awe and wonder at seeing this new person. What kind of adventures await today?

February 28

On this lovely last day of February, breathe in the love that exists all around you. The love between you and your spouse is romantic and sustaining. The love between you and your child is unconditional. The love between you and your family and friends is heartwarming. But the love between you and your soul is essential. Don't wait to start dreaming, scheming, and doing. All things are possible if you have love and respect for yourself and your creativity.

"You can, you should, and if you're brave enough to start, you will." ~Stephen King

MARCH

Spring Cleaning

March 1

Rabbit, Rabbit, Rabbit. A new month. The month that spring arrives!

Spring:
(n). the season after winter and before summer, in which vegetation begins to appear.
(v). to move or jump suddenly or rapidly upward or forward. (Google.com)

New life begins to appear, and movement is inevitable. Feel the hope that this month brings on its pastel, flower filled heels. Spring is so close...so close.

March 2

The element linked to the month of March is *WATER*. The elixir of life. Nourishment. Ice thaws, rivers run again, and snow turns to rain. March is a fluid month, where animals—and people—start to emerge from hibernation to rejoin the world around them. It's the perfect month to wash off the dust on whatever goals you've set for yourself but haven't quite gotten to yet. Choose one today. A new recipe, a closet cleaned, a book started—it can be big or small—but choose one, and get started right now.

Jump in, Mama. The water feels great...

March 3

Spring cleaning guides us through this month. We have to work on letting go of the clutter in ourselves to make room for new thoughts, new attitudes, and new goals. What do you need to "clean out" from your heart...your soul?

Today I let go of my habit of...
Today I let go of my need to control...
Today I let go of my relationship with...
Today I let go of the clutter in...
Today I let go of feeling like...
Today I let go of telling myself...
Today I let go of secretly...

Finish these sentences—and see where your early morning musings take you today.

March 4

The morning greets us with subconscious thoughts. Have you ever consciously opened yourself up to them? Those fragile, random minutes between dreamland and coffee are filled with possibility, spontaneity, and inspiration. The normal habits and boundaries we set for ourselves haven't yet taken hold, and we can be, think, and create whatever reality we want. Cherish these moments. Expand on them. Don't let them drift away as you live—fully present—in this day.

March 5

Check out Boss Babe on Instagram today—these are some optimistic, get sh*t done girls. And I love it.

"Because I want to show her that dreams come true." ~Boss Babe

"Risking is better than regretting." ~Boss Babe

"The first step in being successful is being a professional optimist." ~Boss Babe

See?

March 6

Become an inspiring woman by learning about inspiring women. It is so motivating to read other successful women's stories. It can feed the fire in you.

"Mistakes are a part of the dues one pays for a full life."
"I'd rather drink wine and eat pasta than be a size zero."
~Sophia Loren, mother of two

March 7

"Be a woman other women can trust. Have the courage to tell another woman direct when she has offended, hurt, or disappointed you. Successful women have a loyal tribe of loyal and honest women behind them. Not haters. Not backstabbers or women who whisper behind their back. Be a woman who lifts other women."
~Sophia A. Nelson

Yes. Let's lift other women around us. There is enough success and love and praise and victory and laughter in the universe for all of us. Be the catalyst of positivity and creativity to your tribe today. Be the match that strikes the flame. And burn bright.

March 8

International Women's Day Journal Exercise
Being a woman is magical. Being a woman is lucky. Being a woman is graceful. Being a woman is mysterious. Being a woman is strong. Keep going with this thought process today. Write down the things that you know to be true about being a woman. And then choose three women in your life—that you know personally or not—and write down the characteristics about them that you admire. It's motivating to have mentors in our lives and to aspire to great things like all the brave women who've come before and will come after.

March 9

Today is National Get Over It Day. In honor of that powerful goddess warrior thought, what do you need to get over today? Leaving troubles, anxieties, and jealousies in the past—where they belong!—is one of the healthiest things we can do for ourselves. Carrying too much baggage and regret will only weigh our souls down, when all they truly want to do is soar. Hate early mornings? Get over it. Dislike folding laundry? Get over it! Wish your stomach was flatter? Get over it. Frustrated with yourself for feeling judged or overthinking every tiny thing in a day? Get. Over. It. One second worrying is one second wasted. And we just don't have that kind of time.

March 10

"Little stones that are pelted into the lake of consciousness should not throw the whole lake into commotion." ~Paramahansa Yogananda, <u>God Talks With Arjuna</u>

Oh how I struggle with this and wish I didn't. We work so hard to be calm, to be serene, to be "with it". And then one bad day, one uncomfortable conflict has our whole world upset. To let it ripple and die out would be a relief. One that I look forward to mastering someday.

March 11

Spring cleaning our souls is hard work. People always say just let it go. But until you are ready to truly move on from something, the feelings and baggage will just linger. And each day must be spent practicing letting it go. And when the right time comes, letting go will be possible because of all this practice we've done. So until then, this quote spoke to my mama soul—a mama just trying to be the best woman and role model she can be for her family and friends. Here's to you and your self evolution journey today.

"It's not a matter of letting go—you would if you could. Instead of 'let it go' we should probably say 'let it be.'" ~Jon Kabat -Zinn

March 12

Plant a flower today. The sweet and simple life that you will see every time you pass it will bring a smile to your face. Choose a petal with the color you need to attract in your life. Pink for love, red for passion, yellow for joy. Find a vintage coffee can and set it on your kitchen windowsill and watch life happen. Plant a flower today. Celebrate color. Celebrate growth. Celebrate life.

March 13

"If you wish to make anything grow, you must understand it, and understand it in a very real sense. 'Green fingers' are a fact, and a mystery only to the unpracticed. But green fingers are the extensions of a verdant heart." ~Russell Page, The Education of a Gardener

Parenting is gardening. I worry my thumb is not green enough to get the job done sometimes. I forget that no parent is perfect, and we are all learning as we go. Just like our children. When I finally remind myself of this, it is easier to come to terms with the worry that never really leaves you when you lay your head on your pillow at night. But if we can keep our hearts authentic and pure, and work to truly understand these adorably challenging miracles we have created—we can learn to be better gardeners. And the parenting stuff will follow right behind.

March 14

Routine: a sequence of actions regularly followed; a fixed program. (Oxforddictionaries.com)

Not exactly a breathless with excitement, romantic, or adventurous type of word, right? Ah...routine. Parenting, especially with little ones, can be all about routine. The changing of diapers, the washing dishes, the constantly making food that your kids may or may not eat, the endless worrying if they are sleeping, eating, playing, learning enough. Routine can be a burden, and it can be so soul tiring as the days go by.

But the key to all of this, Mama? The key to all of this is mindfulness. It has to be. It's the only answer that brings spontaneity, magic, and delight back into the routine. Look for the smile on your bebe's face as they find their shadow for the first time. Look for the humor in the smeared faces, the dirty clothes. And for goodness sake, let's stop worrying so much. The day will unfold as it will—loads of laundry and all.

So go attack that routine with joy today. Because sweet and sticky kisses, delightfully childish laughter, and dress up adventures is really what this life is all about.

March 15

The Ides of March. A famous day whether you know what it represents or not. But before Shakespeare made it infamous in <u>Julius Caesar</u>, it was an ancient Roman holiday. March marked the beginning of the new year in the Roman calendar—the 15th being the very first full moon. And so the Romans celebrated Anna Perenna, goddess of the year, and had festivals, picnics, and parties honoring that exceptional time. New year—new possibilities—new adventures. Let's take a page from the Romans, shall we? Have a picnic, toast today, and celebrate life.

March 16

Motivation. It comes in all forms, and you never know how long it's going to stay around. As much as we ride high on the days it finds us, it's not always that effortless. Don't hesitate to seek motivation out. Search out that inspirational flame that is the true seed of life and happiness in all of us. You could find it in music, in art, in the ocean. It could shower you when you finally turn your face up to a sunbeam. Just keep searching.

"People often say that motivation doesn't last. Well neither does bathing. That's why we recommend it daily." ~Zig Ziglar, Author and Motivational Speaker

March 17

The color green represents abundance and fertility. It stimulates growth, success, life, and harmony. Surround yourself with this essence today. Let it restore your soul as you embrace the "Luck o' the Irish'. Hope literally springs eternal. Within your family. Within your friends. Within yourself.

March 18

"It was one of those March days when the sun shines hot and the wind blows cold: when it is summer in the light and winter in the shade." ~Charles Dickens, <u>Great Expectations</u>

I love the cusper months. The in between days. Not too hot, not too cold—with anticipation of farewell to one season and welcome to another. Say a prayer of gratitude wherever you are, right now. For your life, your family, and your chance to experience this beautiful day.

March 19

Speaking of luck this month, fun fact for you: Only one in 10,000 clovers have the lucky four leaves. I love to search for those charmed clovers with my daughter. It's a game of enchantment and adventure we can play almost anywhere. Our very own treasure hunt full of giggles and memories. Start those memories now, Mama...they will stay with you forever.

March 20

Spring. Spring is here. In one cool, refreshing breeze, feel spring wash over you. Feel it cleanse the hibernation of winter away. This is the time for new life, new growth, and new chances. Open your windows, throw open your doors, and greet spring like an old friend come to tea. Or wine.

You choose.

March 21

Do you ever find it overwhelming to write down all your dreams at once in your journal? Sometimes I find it hard to intentionally meditate on all the dreams and goals that I have for myself. The space between where I am now and where I want to be can seem pretty big. In She Means Business, by Carrie Green, she suggests you make a "dream jar". Fill it with individual goals you have and a couple times a day, pull one of those papers out of the jar. Meditate on that one dream for two minutes straight. I love this. It simplifies all the awesome things I want to accomplish, and makes it easier to focus on one at a time.

10 second tip: When you are tired and over a workout or a chore, choose one of those dreams from your jar and say it out loud to yourself as you finish your reps or the dishes. The time will fly by, and you will be filled with determination and excitement!

March 22

Life is filled with good days and bad days. It is imprinted on our minds that we cannot truly enjoy the good unless we have experienced the bad. But honestly what makes a day either good or bad? It seems to be decided by whatever memory leaves the deepest mark. And you, my friend, have the power to decide what will leave the deepest mark. You don't have to let the negative moments take control. You can teach yourself—teach your children—to learn from the bad, but then leave it behind.

What if life is filled with good—and the bad is just a stepping stone that helps us keep on keepin' on...

March 23

"Everything seemed possible, when I looked through the eyes of a child.
And every once in awhile; I remember,
I still have the chance to be that wild."
~Nikki Rowe

Just a sweet, savory, and simply inspiring thought to start your day...

March 24

Ok. Let's get serious with cleansing our souls today, Mama. It's hard, it's messy, and it's uncomfortable—but the bottom line? We all want to be free from bad habits, toxic people, and negative ruts. And we can never achieve true mindfulness, peace, and confidence until we realize that it takes constant work to keep our souls cleansed.

In order to banish toxicity from our lives, we have to figure out *why* they are toxic in the first place. What about these things affect you negatively? Sometimes it's so subtle, we hardly recognize the triggers. And sometimes it's not so much the actions of others, but the deep rooted uneasiness within ourselves that needs to be addressed. Jealousy is the killer of all joy. Comparison is the thief of all contentment. When toxicity invades our lives, we have to stop in that moment and assess why we feel that way. What about the situation is causing those feelings of jealousy, discontent, or yearning? It is in this soul searching that we can learn what is missing in our lives and what areas we need to work on within ourselves. Then those toxic people and moments no longer affect us. And ah...imagine what a freeing, powerful, and truly magical woman you will be when that happens.

March 25

"The moment you doubt whether you can fly, you cease forever to be able to do it."
~J.M. Barrie, <u>Peter Pan</u>

Sometimes a simple reminder of what is at stake in this whole life thing—this whole motherhood thing—this whole woman thing—is a good thing.

March 26

Focus on cleansing your life from the inside out this month. Meditating on the importance of our thoughts is the key to understanding how we invite both good and bad into our lives. What are you reading right now? What are you studying? What enlightening conversation have you had lately? Yes, motherhood can be a lot of toddler talk and not a lot of adult time. So how can we create more inspiration in our daily lives? We have to consciously seek out the moments of personal growth—instead of settling for the ruts that this phase can dig. Work on bringing passion and stimulation into your day. It can be as simple as reading a book, calling a friend, or learning a new skill. And it can be as fantastic as crushing those goals you set for yourself back in January.

Remember them? Revisit them right now.

"The Law of Attraction states that whatever you focus on, think about, read about, and talk about intensely, you're going to attract more of into your life."
~Jack Canfield

March 27

The sunrise is a wonder each morning. Spring is seriously making its appearance with the birds chirping outside my window. They are awfully loud at six am. "Get up! Get up!" they say. Is it a song? Is it like a human conversation? "Timmy! Susie! Get up or you'll be late for school!" As I listen deeper, I can hear different layers of bird song. How far away are some of those birds? Who else is listening to their morning ritual? If the birds can be devoted to their morning ritual, we can be devoted to ours too, right? Don't cheat yourself out of your morning birdsong, Mama. It's essential to begin your day drenched in inspiration. (For some inspiration: see the "Morning Ritual" on January 13th!)

March 28

Spring cleaning is so therapeutic, isn't it? But not just our homes, cars, and closets—let's work on cleaning out our minds and hearts too. The clutter and baggage that sticks around in there is so heavy to carry around. It holds us back. It stunts our growth. It strands us in the past. And that is not what this year is about. So make this your intention for the day...

I am open to letting go of the emotional baggage from this past year.
My heart is clear and free flowing.
I receive fresh and optimistic hope in every moment.
I am renewed and ready for creativity.

March 29

"God gave those little children to you, Mama—You. No one else can mother them like you can. You may have your work cut out for you, but you're the one cut out to accomplish it." ~Erin Odom, The Humbled Homemaker Blog

Let those thoughts empower you to the very core of your soul. You already know this. This life, this phase, this day is a gift from God— and we must not waste it. Don't beat yourself up over mistakes. Just move on and be better each day. Just like we encourage our children, encourage yourself too. We are all growing up together.

March 30

"Do not speak about anyone who is not physically present." ~Allan Lokos, <u>Pocket Peace: Effective Practices for Enlightened Living</u>

I hear a lot of Mamas say they are "taking a break" from social media. Do you notice this? Sometimes we get so addicted to the digital world, we can feel our actual realities start to be affected by it. I think we all need a break from this sometimes. If the constant barrage of other people's lives, problems, triumphs, and lunch choices is taking the place of our lives, problems, triumphs, and lunch choices then we may need to unplug.

Spring Cleaning Challenge
Unplug this week. Do not get on social media right when you wake up. Roll over and spend some quality time with your love instead. Or set some intentions for your day. Or enjoy a cup of coffee, and watch the view outside your window. And keep your social media viewing limited to twice a day. Our human souls were not built to take in so many other people's emotions so often. It can't help but permeate our world. And we are working way too hard to create a magical life to let that happen.

March 31

Terrible days are terrible days. No matter how you slice them. Sometimes we must give in to the dark in order to let the light find some room. If you don't acknowledge your struggles and your demons, you are just pushing them further inside and not forcing them out in the open. It is only when we get them out in the open that we can release them, release ourselves from the power they have over us. What is your demon today? Are you feeling stuck in this pattern of life right now?

When I feel the darkness start to take hold, I go back to the basics. Sweep clean the extra in your life, and work on your soul for a few days. For me, it's journaling every morning to get the cobwebs out, it's working out, it's eating clean. Work on your soul, and your soul will work on you.

APRIL

Planting Seeds

April 1

April. For the next 30 days, it's April. In the Southern Hemisphere it feels like October, so almost anywhere on this planet it is either Fall or Spring. The seasons of balance. Neither too hot nor too cold. I love the highs in life, and I try to grow from the lows—but sometimes the best times are the moments when you can find true balance in your life. And happiness is an equal amount of inspiration, love, and peace. So go out there and find a slice of your happiness today. Shower everyone around you with it. I dare you. Just see how many people you have the power to inspire today.

April 2

"April hath put a spirit of youth in everything." ~William Shakespeare

Channel your inner youth today. Need some inspiration? Just stand back and witness the undeniable joy and curiosity in your children. That free spirit, living in the moment attitude is infectious. Let those beautiful, crazy, frustrating, delightful kiddos teach you something today.

April 3

Get rid of some clutter today. In one area of your life—your car, your inbox, your kitchen counters, your closet—spend a moment spring cleaning. Clutter is like cholesterol; it clogs and weighs us down on a daily basis. Don't keep passing over those things that stress you out every day. Just. Get. Rid. Of. It. The air you take in your lungs after a good de-cluttering session is deep and crisp and delightful...

...Make space for the inspiring, Mama.

April 4

How can we better communicate with our kids today? Instead of the generic "how was your day?" or "what did you do at school today?", ask them about their peaks and valleys. It opens up a raw and honest way for them to be real with you. They can share the confident parts and the vulnerable parts in a way that is safe for them. I have already tried this with my two-and-a-half-year-old; and while she barely understands what this means, I can already see the wheels turning. I can see the seeds being planted to be able to come to her mama and share her journey. Her peak may be the cupcake she got to eat at preschool, but hey, it's the small stuff, right? Start those seeds of communication early...and then let's watch them grow together.

April 5

Powerful Woman Alert! I must be living under a rock, because I only recently discovered Brene Brown. Wow. What an incredible woman. If you are looking for some inspiration, look up her Ted Talks on vulnerability. So much food for thought packed into 20 minutes. You won't regret it!

"Many of us will spend our entire lives trying to slog through the shame swampland to get to a place where we can give ourselves permission to both be imperfect and to believe we are enough." ~Brene Brown

April 6

"The flower doesn't dream of the bee. It blossoms and the bee comes." ~Mark Nepo, Poet and Philosopher

Let's not wait one more second for joy to find us. For growth to happen. For someone or something to validate us. Blossom first. Have courage to simply be happy. To be content. To be whole. Imagine the lessons your children will learn from seeing a whole hearted, vulnerable, and authentic mama. The power is ours.

April 7

Today is National Beer Day and National No Housework Day. I don't know why that cracks me up. I can definitely get behind the spirit of this. Who's with me?

April 8

What are you waking up to today? For just a moment—wherever you are—look around you. Take in your surroundings. Most days blur by in a chorus of kids, work, chores, hopefully something fun, and repeat. We scarcely notice the bedroom walls or the view outside the kitchen window. But if we can just take a few moments to notice the pretty flowers blooming or the hazy light that filters into our bedroom at dawn, we can breathe and give thanks for the sweet blessing of another day.

April 9

"After all, Ginger Rogers did everything that Fred Astaire did. She just did it backwards and in high heels." ~Anne Richards, American Politician, 45th Governor of Texas

I literally repeat this to myself when a wave of nostalgia for my old life or jealousy of my husband's work trips sneak up on me. We. Are. Rockstars. Keep creating today...keep chasing those dreams. Your kids and your soul and yes, your husband, will thank you for it.

April 10

The word April stems from the Latin word *aperit* which means to open. A perfect time to work on opening your heart and mind to the possibilities and opportunities that this month brings. What areas or ideas could you open up to today? Most times the things I feel myself shying away from or avoiding are the very things I need to accept and experience. I really can't say I've ever regretted trying something new or conquering a fear. Can you?

April 11

Our goal as parents is to plant the seeds within our children that will help them grow into loving, dream chasing, confident humans. Every day it is our duty to make sure these enchanting little souls have the freedom and the safety they need to discover who they are, who they want to be, and what their connection is to this big and beautiful world.

"Connection is the energy that is created between people when they feel seen, heard, and valued - when they can give and receive without judgement." ~Brene Brown

April 12

"If you want something you've never had, you must be willing to do something you've never done." ~Thomas Jefferson

I woke up this morning full of fire and energy to create the life I always dream of. This motivation is crucial to getting out of my comfort zone and attacking my goals with courage and fearlessness. In order to get where we want to go, we have to be willing to do scary things. And what is the worst that could happen? Someone says no? We can always just ask someone else. But what if—*oh what if!*—the answer is yes?

Start by saying yes to yourself today. Right now. Go after a goal or an inspiring whim. Say yes. And watch your dreams begin to come true.

April 13

Guys. We are moms. We are parents. We are raising humans every single day. And each day I can't help but feel like I'm still raising myself sometimes. I swear my kid teaches me more about life than I am teaching her.

Some mornings I struggle to find the inspiration to be the mindful mom, wife, and friend that I want to be. It is still hard for me to accept that this is okay. The whole point of inspiration is that you have to seek it out. You have to search for it, and accept it. Motivation doesn't just wait patiently for you to pluck it out of the air when you need it. Like all good things, you have to work for it. And if you are open to inspiration, to magic, to happiness, I promise you will find it. Perhaps it is even closer than you thought.

"But what if you are the light? What if you're the very agent of illumination that a dark situation begs for?" ~Elizabeth Gilbert, Writer

April 14

"There are always flowers for those that want to see them." ~Henri Matisse, Artist

Attitude will make or break our daily journey through motherhood. How do we keep the peaceful, positive, and powerful tone we set for ourselves this morning last all day long? It's simple. We choose. We decide to see the flowers. And we see them. Happy people attract happiness. Negative people attract sadness. Moody people attract chaos. Distracted people attract disrespect. What do you choose to attract today?

April 15

We can do this. We can do this foggy, sleep deprived, routine drenched, motherhood thing. I promise. We were strong enough to create these beautiful souls, and we can be strong enough to stay positive and inspired in this time of haziness. We just have to believe it and take it all one day at a time. All the while determined to not lose ourselves in the process.

Radical self care. Determined sense of humor. Unfailing search for gratitude.

Those three things sustain us, Mama. We are strong enough.

April 16

Let your heart be like a gate in a garden. Always opening and closing with the breeze. You must let joy in and out, you must let pain in and out. Free like the breeze. Free.

"The truth is everything will be okay as soon as you are okay with everything. That is the only time everything will be okay." ~Michael Singer, <u>The Untethered Soul</u>

April 17

"To be worthy does not mean to be perfect." ~Gerrit W. Gong

Ah, I needed to hear this today. Perhaps we don't always have to be perfect. Perhaps we can teach our little ones that imperfect is nothing to be ashamed of. That the meaning is in the effort and the heart and the intention we put into each and every day. It is such an interesting and unnatural thought to give ourselves the grace to just be. To accept that life will go as planned sometimes, and then go totally wrong the next. But how we navigate the highs and lows are the tools that truly matter. Let's tear down the facades we've created...and let's show the world what it is to be worthy.

April 18

Root:
(n) *the basic cause, source, or origin of something.*
(v) *establish deeply and firmly. (Google.com.)*

As I watch my family grow and encourage us to thrive these days, I cannot help but think about roots. These days, families are spread out across the globe; it's easy to see how some of us feel unsettled. We always hear about people who are lost, drifting through life—and how they "get back to their roots" to try to find themselves. Our roots let us live, provide nourishment, and make us strong. If you don't feel connected to the Earth, to your life, then how can you encourage yourself to fly? We have to grow down so that we can grow up, Mama. So work on your roots today. Get connected to your community and your tribe, so that you can be as strong and as everlasting as the tallest Oak Tree.

Root Down Journal Exercise
Spend a few moments today brainstorming ways you can feel more rooted in your life. How can you get involved in your community? Church. Yoga. An art class. Visit your local Farmer's Market. And above all, who can you reach out to and spend some time with? A coffee date or a facetime session with your people can fill the soul in amazing ways.

April 19

"Maybe you are searching in the branches for what only appears in the roots."
~Rumi

Think about it. If we live among the branches we can be swayed by the smallest gust of wind, only to bend back the other way when nature changes her mind. But if we work to stand our ground, know our truth, and get rooted in our lives, then the whims of change cannot break us. There is no need to fear the wind. Instead, let it refresh you and teach you, so you can teach others how to bend without breaking as well.

April 20

I woke up this morning craving nature. I'd left a kitchen window open the night before and could hear birds singing as I enjoyed the few minutes before mama duties set in. We don't have to be "outdoor people" to enjoy the fresh breeze on our cheeks, the smell of the ocean, the mountains, or a garden. Take a nature walk with your family today. Notice the animals, watch the birds fly, listen to the sound of nature—a sound that's been around much much longer than the clicking of a keyboard or the ding of a text message. Step outside—step outside *yourself*—and see what wonders are around you today.

April 21

What kind of mama do you want your babes to see today? The whimsical one? The spontaneous one? The creative one? The child at heart one? Right now, you have the awesome task of raising your babies to be functioning adults. Interesting adults, compassionate adults, driven and inspiring adults. The person they will become starts with the mom they see right now. So have a picnic on the living room floor, get messy in the kitchen, take them somewhere fun and create something.

That Mom is the one they'll remember, the one they'll be shaped by, and the one that makes all the difference.

April 22

Why is it so hard to stay happy and inspired? Why is it so easy to get frustrated or disappointed? When life is good, man is it sweet. But when it's not? When the baby isn't napping, or there is trouble at school, or you feel like a broken record of no's and cleaning and laundry—a day can feel like a year. It is these days that we have to fight back against. These days where you need your arsenal of motivation. These are the days you just have to "slap some lipstick on" and keep swimming.

If you feel yourself sliding down that slope of blah—stop. Wherever you are, just stop. Close your eyes. Slow your breath and listen. Listen to the air, to your heartbeat, to the screaming child in the background. Whatever feeling is choking you or making you feel anxious—bring it to the center of your mind. With each inhale acknowledge that thought, with each exhale let that thought go. Like a balloon floating free, send that stress away. Repeat until your heart unlocks and the heaviness lifts. Then spread a smile on your face and get back to living, Mama. You got this. Don't let the bad get you down.

April 23

Today is National Picnic Day. The perfect excuse to step outside and let fresh air and soulful sunshine do their work to wash away the stress of the day. To kids, picnics are whimsical. They are an adventure. They are a delightful excuse to make a mess and play, play, play. Sounds utterly delicious, doesn't it?

April 24

We are very much into spring now. The season for rebirth, growth, possibility. Positivity is a mindset—one we have to work on every single day. We must start to expect good things to happen to us. We have to be open to dreams coming true; in fact, believing that they already have. These kinds of positive affirmations truly change our brain waves and begin to attract all the goals and passions and creativity we want in our lives.

"Expect your every need to be met, expect the answer to every problem, expect abundance on every level, expect to grow spiritually." ~Eileen Caddy, Spiritual Teacher

This is not just thinking something and expecting it to magically appear. It is consciously banishing the negative thoughts that inevitably creep in to hold us back and simply going after what we want. It is possible, Mama. And springtime is the time to believe it.

April 25

Unfurl: *make or become spread out from a rolled or folded state, especially in order to be open to the wind. (Google.com)*

As we sink our fingers into the depths of spring and plant the seeds for the rest of the year, there comes a time when you have to sit back and be patient. To wait for your flowers to grow. Patience is a virtue, but it does not mean you do nothing during this waiting period. No, you must cultivate the spark inside of you. So as you wait, continue to stoke the flame inside by meditating, journaling, yoga-ing, and saying your positive affirmations every single day. You want to be prepared when the time comes to unfurl your petals and release all the wonder and beauty that is undeniably you.

April 26

Planting Seeds Journal Exercise
Spend a few minutes today finishing the following sentences...

The most surprising goal I set for myself this year is...
The goal I most want to accomplish this year is...
When I think about accomplishing my goals I feel...
Today I will do_____ to help get me to my goal.

These goals you are racing toward, they are the seeds of inspiration and creative living that you have planted. Waiting for them to grow can be tedious, and it is easy to get lost or forget the whys behind your desires. Remember the whys, Mama. And don't let them go.

April 27

"Often I'll go outside and just place my hands on the soil, even if there's no work to do on it. When I am filled with worries, I do that and I can feel the energy of the mountains and of the trees." ~Andy Couturier, <u>A Different Kind of Luxury: Japanese Lessons in Simple Living and Inner Abundance</u>

We all need tips and tricks to bring us back to ourselves when life spins out of control. What are your tricks? Is it ten deep breaths? Is it dancing in the kitchen to your favorite 90's jam? Is it stopping and finding a positive spin or affirmation to whatever the situation is? Perhaps it's stepping outside and letting Mother Nature remind us that whatever we are facing, it is not as big a deal as we think it is. Yes, our problems can seem massive and terrifying, but if we can just gain a little perspective with the rest of the world, perhaps those problems can seem a bit more manageable. Let the earth remind you that miracles happen. Everywhere…and all the time.

April 28

A dream starts in the soul. It is the seed that life, passion, and purpose springs forth from. You will know when you are on the right path—when you are following your heart—when you are living your creative truth. You will know it. Deep down in your soul.

"When you do things from your soul, you feel a river moving in you. A joy."
~Rumi

Follow that joy. Let that river flow within you. Movement is a good thing. It means evolvement. It means hope. It means happiness.

April 29

At times the winds of motherhood change and take our breath away. Are you ever struck down with a longing for your old life? A picture, an old friend, being confronted with an old dream that didn't quite pan out. These tricky storms can upend our normal paths and leave us breathless with the status of our lives. Being a mom is hard. It's ok to say that. Say it out loud. Being a mom is hard. It is natural to miss parts of our old lives, and it is healthy to be able to look back on that life and be brave enough to admit you miss it sometimes.

Ride the waves of motherhood. It's the only thing you can do when the storm breaks. There is hope in tomorrow, and family truly is the greatest thing in the world. Nothing can change that—even you.

Quick fix: Sneak in your little one's room while they sleep and take a peek. Your heart will swell and every anxiety will dissipate like a dandelion blowing in the breeze. Sweetest. Thing. Ever. (Just don't wake them up! For the love of everything holy, don't wake them up :)).

April 30

> *"If I accept sunshine and warmth, then I must also accept thunder and lightning."* ~Kahlil Gibran, Writer, Poet, Artist

We take the good with the bad. The sweet with the sour. The hot and the cold. Everything has a yin and yang to it in this world, and we might as well get comfortable with that now. It would be impossible to truly enjoy the high moments in our lives without knowing what the lows are like. And that's what we need to pass on to our children too. How to navigate the ebb and flow in life...how to face the storms with bravery and determination. A good April thunderstorm can bring passion and drama, can't it? Some of the darkest parts of my story are when the brightest dreams were born. Which means there is always hope, Mama. There is always hope.

MAY

Growth

The Daily Soul Sessions For Every Mama

May 1

Another new start. Remember how May used to feel growing up? The excitement as the end of the school year came and summer was so close you could taste it? Lemonade, lazy pool days, hot sunshine, horseback rides, stolen kisses, and new romances. The anticipation of summer is one of my favorite times of the year. It's just brimming with possibility and adventure. Take a moment this morning—journal, meditate, be creative for a minute—and think about what this time of year meant to you as a child. Bring it to life today. Take that excitement for unknown adventure with you as you live this lovely first day of May.

"The world's favorite season is the spring. All things seem possible in May."
~Edwin Way Teale, Naturalist and Photographer

May 2

Sometimes it is nice to get out of your routine for a while. Go on a vacation, take a drive, leave the comfort of your home and see a different part of the world—or even your neighborhood. Being a mom can bring out the control freak in each of us, and it ain't always pretty. Have you convinced yourself that if bebe gets off her schedule, the world could possibly end? As much as my little one thrives on naps, snacks, and playtime, I'm always amazed at how resilient she is. How adaptable. Get inspired by the joy that spontaneity brings your kids. Maybe we can find that joy today, too. Outside of the box, Mama. Live outside of the box.

May 3

It is that time of year again. The time to celebrate mothers. Spring time. Baby time. New life time. Mama time. Don't let this delightful excuse to celebrate *you* go unnoticed. Celebrate with your family, but celebrate with yourself, too. At some point this week take some time to give yourself a gift. Take yourself on a date, schedule a drink with a friend. Take a painting class, curl up with a great book, or get your nails done in a fantastically female color. Do something you've been wanting to. Celebrate you, Mama. You are worth it.

May 4

Life is filled with signs. They're everywhere, pointing us in different directions, subtly influencing our decisions throughout any given day. Do you pay attention to them? Do you pray for them? I can get so caught up in my own crazy life that sometimes I forget to open my eyes and receive the signs that I ask for. A song, a butterfly, a word that just keeps popping up everywhere you go—these are the signs that we need to be aware of. They have meaning. They have power. It's the universe giving us a little nudge, a little "keep going, girl, you're on the right path..." Don't be afraid to say out loud what you want out of this day, and then watch the world—and yourself—make it happen. I'm constantly delighted at the way signs show up...when you least expect them...and perhaps when you need them the most.

"Wonders and Signs are miracles of God." ~Lailah Gifty Akita, Founder of Smart Youth Volunteers Foundation

May 5

"I think that the power is the principle. The principle of moving forward, as though you have the confidence to move forward, eventually gives you confidence when you look back and see what you've done." ~Robert Downey, Jr.

Take. That. Step. The first one. The first one is always the hardest. But nothing was ever accomplished without someone taking the first step. The first risk. The first breath. And that first step will lead you to the next, and the next, and the next. And before you know it, you are so much more, so much further on your journey to whatever goal you want to accomplish. Then you can *"look back and see what you've done"*...and that is delightful.

May 6

Parenting is hard. Everyone has a different style of discipline, and learning what style works best for you and your family is challenging. "Because I said so" wants to slip off my tongue so badly sometimes, it's shocking. But our kids don't deserve such narrow and closed off communication. They deserve authenticity and thoughtful reasons as to why we say the things we say. Strict does not have to mean stunted. Communication wins every time.

May 7

"We are born in one day.
We die in one day.
We can change in one day.
And we can fall in love in one day.
Anything can happen in just one day."
~Gayle Forman, Author

This. Just this. Don't take for granted this day. It's all ours. And it is what we make of it.

May 8

May is a hopeful month. Even the word, May...conjures up possibility, different paths, and opportunities. The word itself means:

Expressing Possibility
Expressing Permission (Google.com)

I love that. This month—this word—is all about coming up with the dream and then giving yourself permission to follow it. To go after the desires of your soul. You may begin to dream...

...starting now...

May 9

Vulnerable Journal Exercise

You have to recognize your weaknesses in order to become better. Become stronger. Weaknesses are not bad, they are simply the aspects in us that might need a little extra TLC from time to time. Try this exercise: Make a—short!—list of a few vulnerabilities you know you possess. Get real with yourself, don't hold back. Your true soul already knows the areas that need some work. But then, before you finish this exercise, across the page change the sentence to a positive affirmation. So where one side says...

I hate confrontation.

The other side could say...

I speak my mind and heart to strengthen my relationships.

Just try this. By putting a mindful and positive spin on our vulnerability we can begin to be more powerful, well rounded, and fascinating women.

"Out of your vulnerabilities will come your strength." ~Sigmund Freud

May 10

I want to live in the moment. What I mean by this is I want to appreciate the season or phase that I find myself in, and not spend my life wishing my way to the next moment, the next nap time, the next holiday. It seems we begin to learn this annoying habit when we are growing up. Wishing to turn 16, waiting for Friday, wanting that boy to ask us to the Prom—we just willingly ask time to pass faster and faster—and guess what? Time obliges us. By the time we have our own children a year seems to literally fly by like a shooting star. You can completely miss the beauty if you don't open your eyes and go looking for it. Let's go look for life today. Just look for it. Notice the flowers, delight in your babe's laughter, stop and really enjoy your husband's kiss as you part ways this morning. Look for life in the moments that you are creating today. They are all that are guaranteed anyway. Might as well enjoy them.

May 11

Let's go down the rabbit hole of living in the season of your life today. It's spring. Spring means new life, planting gardens, and having babies. Experience this season in all its hopeful glory. Buy the fruits and veggies that are in season, visit the zoo because the babies are being born, plant your herb garden and enjoy tending it with your family. Teach them to appreciate the seasons of their lives by enjoying this beautiful season we are in today.

"A garden is a grand teacher. It teaches patience and careful watchfulness; it teaches industry and thrift; above all it teaches entire trust." ~Gertrude Jekyll, British Horticulturist and Writer

...Kind of like being a parent, eh?

May 12

Life can get a little lonely sometimes. Raising kids is the most exciting, the most time consuming, the most surprising, the most rewarding, and the most boring thing. And oh so lonely sometimes. Statisticbrain.com says there are 85.4 million mothers in the US alone—and yet...and yet. There is nothing quite so lonely as a temper tantrum in Target, or a 3am wake up call for the millionth day in a row. Why is that? Why do we feel alone even during a playdate with a good friend and their kids? Is it because we all raise our children differently? We are all unique, and that can be a little lonely. And we just have to learn to live with it. To make the best of it. To not see it as so negative—but to invite that feeling into our lives, so we can move past it to the rewarding, the surprising, the exciting parts of mamahood.

> *"A lonely day is God's way of saying that he wants to spend some quality time with you."* ~Criss Jami, Killosophy

May 13

Grow: (of a living thing) to undergo natural development by increasing in size and changing physically; progress to maturity. (Google.com)

This month is the month for growth. We've planted the seeds of spring, and now we start to witness the maturity and change around us. It's an excellent time to take a moment to mindfully come back to areas in your life that you wish for growth.

Journal Exercise
Use your journal time to be honest with yourself, and reassess your goals for self growth. Health, motherhood, relationships, love, responsibility, new skills, hobbies...in what ways have you succeeded, and in what areas could you dedicate more effort?

May 14

Have you been to your yoga mat lately? I find my body is the first thing to get put on the back burner these days amidst chores, work, husband, and kiddos. And what is completely ironic is as soon as I stop working on myself—my body—many times other parts of my life stop working so well. Things stagnate. Stop flowing. Creativity comes to a standstill, and I am not as happy as I know I can be. When this happens, I have to find my yoga mat immediately. I need five minutes, ten tops, to do a simple meditation, complete a hip opening restorative session, or say a prayer. And it helps every time. Without fail, it helps. It opens my breath, lightens my load, brings me back my center...my creativity...myself.

May 15

Acceptance. Acceptance. Acceptance. Sometimes this is all the mantra you need in a day. Let the waves of inspiration, frustration, indifference wash over you...accept them. Acknowledge them. Release them. Hang onto what helps, let go of what hurts, and take a purifying breath in. As mothers, as women, our minds can fill so quickly with busy work and to do lists. My brain gets so fuzzy I forget to take time for myself, and self care is an essential and vital part of being a good mama. Accept yourself, accept this day...Accept.

May 16

"There are two gifts we should give our children. One is roots, and the other is wings." ~Hodding Carter

It is Love A Tree Day. There is so much we can learn from a tree. From its roots, from its branches, from its ability to lose all of its leaves only to grow new ones each year. A tree sways with the breeze, but its roots grow so deep that it cannot be moved. We should look at life this way. We should learn and grow and definitely change a little from the new experiences we have—those experiences are our branches. But just like the roots of a tree, we should always keep our feet planted firmly in the beliefs we know to be true. And never ever be scared to change or lose a few leaves to make room for new ones to grow.

May 17

Set some goals for yourself today. What areas of your life need some attention? Mini goals keep me in the right mindset for feeling creative and free. Perhaps it's a goal to do a five minute meditation during naptime every day this week. Or whenever that TV is on, get on the floor and stretch out your hips to release tension and keep emotions flowing. Maybe it's a goal to go to bed with a clean kitchen, or perhaps consciously make time to kiss your love goodbye in the mornings. Whatever it is, reaching these mini goals bring satisfaction and confidence to your day. And we all deserve more confidence in this world. Confidence is powerful. Confidence is sexy. Confidence is inspiring.

May 18

Apparently it's National No Dirty Dishes Day today. Hallelujah. I do not yet know if this means we are allowed to use paper products all day, the dishes just magically get washed by elves, or our husbands are on cleaning duty...

Who comes up with this stuff? It's gold, people. Gold.

May 19

Pandora Inspiration
Set your channel to Disney (Children's) Radio. I dare you not to start reliving your childhood. Whether or not the babes are in the room, you'll be dancing before you know it.

> *"Do a loony-goony dance*
> *'Cross the kitchen floor,*
> *Put something silly in the world*
> *That ain't been there before."*
> ~Shel Silverstein, <u>A Light in the Attic</u>

May 20

The longer I am a mother, the easier I am able to see how temporary the phases of my life are. Do you notice this, Mama? Sleepless nights, bad moods, teething, terrible twos—it's all temporary. It all passes. Some days we just have to keep telling ourselves this over and over because during the bad phases? A day can feel like a month, and you cannot see the light at the end of the tunnel.

But just as we can have faith that the bad will pass, we also must never take the good for granted. Those long naps, happy smiles, and positive restaurant outings or plane flights are something to be so very grateful for. It's the light, Mama. It's all worth it for the light.

May 21

Try to keep the world at bay for a few moments this morning. Sometimes I get connected almost the second my eyes open. Instead of enjoying my solitude or my sleep, I'm immediately thrown into the chaotic world of email, Instagram, Twitter, and Facebook. Other people's lives, that is. How can we figure out our day or our feelings if we are constantly being bombarded by everyone else's? Don't rush your morning away, Mama. Take a few moments and just be with yourself. Your story. Your truth. What energy and life do you want to bring to this day? The world can wait—your morning won't.

"Don't be satisfied with stories, how things have gone with others. Unfold your own myth." ~Rumi, The Essential Rumi

May 22

Do you ever feel stuck? The routine of motherhood makes my creative spirit feel that way sometimes. It's hard for me to get out of my "mommy head" and into my "artist head". Perhaps it's the spilled peanut butter sticking to my shirt or the 3 piles of unfolded laundry staring me in the face (you know they'll just wrinkle again if you leave them there, ugh!). Nevertheless, we have to get unstuck! The trick is doing something out of your routine, lady. Something you've never done before. Take a walk somewhere you've never been, light a hundred candles in your living room, do a somersault and sing your favorite show tune at the top of your lungs. Or just slap some makeup on, and go have an espresso like they do in Italy—do something for you. I promise the creativity will return if you aren't afraid to get creative first.

May 23

"Success is not final, failure is not fatal: it is the courage to continue that counts."
~Winston Churchill

Whatever happened yesterday, whatever happens today—enjoy this journey. Little triumphs and perseverance are what make us strong, beautiful, and inspiring women. And teaching our families to find the "courage to continue" is what makes us strong, beautiful, and inspiring mothers.

May 24

Meditation: Opening up Heart Energy
Spend a few minutes today opening up the stagnant emotion that is trapped inside you. Some days are more overwhelming than others. Some days you just feel blocked. Some days you need to "take a breather", and find freedom to get your energy moving again.

Close your eyes. Begin alternate nostril breathing: Raise your right hand with your palm facing you, and lower your middle and pointer fingers. Close your left nostril with your ring finger, and breath in through your right nostril. Pause for just a moment at the top of the breath. Then close the right nostril with your thumb, and breathe out through your left side. Breathe in again on the left side, and pause for a moment at the top. Close the left nostril and breathe out on the right side. Repeat this weaving of the breath for five minutes as you feel yourself growing lighter, the breath coming easier. At the end, lower your hand and sit quietly for a few moments. Observe how the energy is moving within you, and find the gratitude in the simplicity of the breath. Your breath.

May 25

Well it's National Wine Day. So there's that.

Spread some cheer and enjoy a glass of your favorite vino. It's a holiday after all.

May 26

Perfect: having all the required or desirable elements, qualities, or characteristics; as good as it is possible to be. (Google.com)

Perfect. What a silly, unattainable word. Perfect. It's a tad boring, a tad snotty, and a tad frustrating. Let's throw that word out the window today and Just. Be. Ourselves. Free, fun, spontaneous...imperfect for a change. Because what makes you you and what makes me me is made up of a million differences and delights. Who wants to boil all that down until we can't tell the difference between the two? Overcooked equals limp and chewy. Al dente is always better—there is a slight bite to it! Letting go of perfection has to be one of the most freeing things we can do. So instead of striving for perfect today, let's strive for authentic, hard-working, inspiring...

...Need I go on?

May 27

Grow today, mama. Our children are everyday examples of undeniable growth—as awkward or fast as it may seem at times. A few pains come with it, but we learn so much along the way. The parts of our lives that we avoid or don't want to think about are the areas that we could use the most growth in. And in order to be better mothers, better people, better women, we have to push ourselves out of our comfort zones. We have to push ourselves spiritually, relationally, in business, and when following our creative passions. So don't fear the growing pains—face them. Let's embrace the growth and see where it takes us.

May 28

It's not always easy to practice self-care, to find the time to journal and meditate. So when it feels hard, it feels *hard*. Do you ever feel stagnant in the stage of life you're in? It's almost a waiting. Waiting for your baby to sleep through the night. Waiting for your toddler to come out of the sleep regression, terrible two phase she's in. Waiting for the workouts to work and the baby weight to disappear. Waiting for your goals to be met. Enough. WAITING.

All the steps are being taken to keep this train moving in the right direction, so why do we dwell on this in between stage? Life is happening now, Girl. Best get to living it.

> *"Be still my love. Open up your heart.*
> *Let the light shine in.*
> *Don't you understand I already have a plan*
> *I'm waiting for my real life to begin."*
> ~Colin Hay, "Waiting For My Real Life To Begin"

May 29

"May and June. Soft syllables, gentle names for the two best months in the garden year: cool, misty mornings gently burned away with a warming spring sun, followed by breezy afternoons and chilly nights. The discussion of philosophy is over; it's time for work to begin." ~Peter Loewer, <u>The Wild Gardener</u>

The discussion of philosophy is over; it's time for work to begin. I love this. This is my mantra as spring slides to summer. Enough thinking and start doing. Write down your goals again this week. Take the steps you need to take to make them happen. Goals with your kids, your husband, your home, your body, your closet, your best friend, your kitchen. Start living that badass, powerful, inspirational, and peaceful life you want to.

May 30

"Deep in their roots, all flowers keep the light." ~Theodore Roethke, Poet

I loved this. True happiness glows from within. If it is only on the surface—superficial and fleeting—you can tell. And it will never sustain, never last. Figure out what lights you up, and follow that path. Glow from within today, Mama.

May 31

"Wherever God has put you, that is your vocation. It is not what we do, but how much love we put into it." ~Mother Teresa

And just like that, May is over, and a new month is about to begin. Don't give this day to anything other than love. Be confident in your choices. Be confident in your life. Be confident that you are right where you are supposed to be.

JUNE

Igniting Passion

June 1

Honor the earth, honor springtime, honor yourself, and celebrate National Barefoot Day today. The ground below us has energy to share—it is brimming with life, wisdom, and strength. To feel the grass, the sand, the dirt beneath our skin transfers that power into us. Channel your inner child today, and get outside with your babes. Try Mountain Pose, and stand up tall with both feet planted firmly on the ground. Or perhaps try Tree Pose, and balance on one leg with your raised foot pressed against your calf and your arms in prayer position or spread up and out like branches in the sky. Inhale and exhale this ever changing yet steadfast world.

June 2

Ahh. A new month. A new adventure. A new phase. Life is a continuous study in recharging and regenerating, isn't it? How do we thrive within our goals, stay in the thick of motherhood, and continue to see every day with joy and possibility—not "here we go again". Children are so good at living in the moment. I read somewhere that kids help us to slow down and enjoy the simple things. And it is so true. We have to enjoy the simple things. A beautiful spring morning. A whimsical backyard wind chime. A delicious breakfast out on a delightful patio. Reading a good book. Simple. Fun. Happy.

In your morning journal, write down at least five simple things you can do this week to add some spice, adventure, passion, or magic to your day. Plan for success, Mama. You are so worth it.

June 3

You are the inspiration, the motivation, the magic for your family. This is the most creative job in the world. Raising new humans and being the strength, the core, the adventure for these new souls is a lot to take on. It's not easy. But it's all about finding creativity. And it's all about staying mindful—in the moment—and present with yourself and your family. The Dalai Lama said:

"Give the ones you love wings to fly, roots to come back, and reasons to stay."

If we can tap into that mantra today, and create a world for ourselves that encourages roots and applauds wings, then we are doing a pretty flipping fantastic job, Mama.

June 4

I have the most wonderful memories of summertime growing up. Our neighborhood, freedom, the heat, endless adventures. Sometimes I feel overwhelmed from trying to recreate that childhood for my own kids. Our world looks a whole lot different now than the one I grew up in, and I have to consciously remind myself that just because my kid's childhood won't be the same as mine does not mean that is a bad thing. Whether or not you liked your childhood doesn't matter, Mama. What matters is this day. This summer. Journal today, paint, sketch—get creative and make a bucket list of 10 things you want to introduce yourself and your family to this summer. Start creating those magical memories right now, and you'll be talking about them for a lifetime.

June 5

"By thinking that everything is black and white, we sometimes close off the way of grace and growth." ~Pope Francis

Whew. Parenthood is no joke. Just when you think you've found one way to parent that seems to be working, your lovely little precious (sometimes I think of them as mini dictators in our household) bebe lets you in on a little secret: raising a child is not black and white. It's a rollercoaster, a test, a freefall, a marathon. And we better get on board and learn to love every messy bit of it because it is in that appreciation—that letting go of control—that we can find grace and growth. These little ones can teach us so so so so so much about life. It's AWEsome.

So go make pancakes, take a nature walk, plant some flowers, do summery stuff. Get busy enjoying the growth today. Be an inspiring example to the world...and to yourself.

June 6

This is the sixth month of the year. The halfway point.

Halfway: *in the middle between two points; not total or complete. (Merriam-Webster.com)*

Phew. Thank goodness. We are halfway through this year, but we don't have to be at the finish line yet. Which gives us the freedom to fall in love with our journey today. Whatever phase you find your soul in—fall in love with your life today.

June 7

June's element is the *EARTH*. Life is bursting out of the ground and the sun is literally baking the grass, sand, and dirt beneath your feet. It's a month to be outside running around with your children and your spouse—soaking in the pleasures that this one precious Earth has to offer us. It's a month to play in your garden, to plant more flowers, to open up your windows and welcome the sounds of the Earth inside. Show gratitude for this immense ball of molecules and atoms that we spin around the sun on. And let's start teaching our children now how important it is to love the world they live in.

June 8

Make someone's day today. Send an email or a letter to an old or cherished friend—just because. Let them know how much they have meant to you, your favorite memory of them, or what you admire about them. I feel like I don't express my love for the friends I have the honor to have. And unless we tell the ones we love why we love them, they'll never know. And that means we are missing the point of this whole life thing.

June 9

What kind of garden, home, or world are we creating for our family today? We all get to choose. What are you leaving out? What are you letting in? Choose wisely, Mama. Our children are watching and learning from us.

June 10

Giving in. I woke up this brand new morning thinking about those words (as I struggled to give in to the pillows and fall blissfully back to sleep...). What does that phrase mean to you? Is it a weak phrase or a strong one? Is it brave or cowardly? I think it's both. It could be giving in to pressure one day but giving in to love the next. It's a form of letting go and a path to moving forward in whatever direction you're pulled in. It's movement. So in this way, giving in is a good thing.

The one thing I still am not quite comfortable *giving in* to? Who I want to be when I grow up. Yes—I said it. None of us have grown up yet, and we are all a work in progress until the day we are no longer here. This is the best news I could possibly hear today, Mama. Now we have a brand new lovely month to continue getting to whoever that grown up person is. I am so much more today than who I was yesterday, and I will be so much more tomorrow. That's an idea I can *give in* to.

"Above all, be the heroine of your life..." ~Nora Ephron

June 11

Today I ignite and invite passion into my life.
Today I ignite and invite sensuality into my life.
Today I ignite and invite confidence into my life.
Today I ignite and invite mystery into my life.
Today I ignite and invite clarity into my life.
Today I ignite and invite self love into my life.
Today I ignite and invite forgiveness into my life.
Today I ignite and invite determination into my life.

June 12

Living a creative life is not easy. We must constantly be pushing ourselves and testing ourselves to go farther, to dream bigger. We must conquer our fears of trying new things and going out on yet another limb. We must learn to see failures as stepping stones and be willing to grow with every challenge. We must not let the haters get to us, but go confidently and joyfully in the direction of what sets our soul afire. Living a creative life is not easy, Mama. But it is magical.

"Being a candle is not easy: in order to give light, one must burn first." ~Rumi

Be a light today. Run after the heat, the burn—and be a light.

June 13

"A rose can never be a sunflower, and a sunflower can never be a rose. All flowers are beautiful in their own way, and that's like women too." ~Miranda Kerr

Coming upon this quote was the sweetest breath of fresh air today. I am flooded with peace and gratitude knowing that we are all different. We all make different choices and live our lives in different ways. And that is beautiful. And magical. And oh so inspiring. I can learn so much from all the women in my life—thank goodness for that.

June 14

Phases, phases, phases. Everything in life has a phase. The moon, the seasons, infancy, toddlerhood, teenage years. Everything in life has a phase. And each phase is simply part of the process of this life. It is the window of time that gets us where we're goin'. So if everything is truly temporary, then why waste one second worrying or wishing time away? The trick is learning how to accept, enjoy, and learn from every moment we get the gift of experiencing. It's all a phase, Mama…it's all a phase.

Phase: A stage in a process of change or development. (Dictionary.com)

June 15

This is the month we celebrate fathers. Dads that are strong, capable, helpful, and fun. I mean sure, 75% of the time they may drive us completely and totally nuts, but is there anything as romantic and attractive as a dad in action? Playing, wrestling, riding bikes, feeding, even changing a diaper can become the sexiest thing in the world to a mama. My my how times have changed.

June 16

Tomorrow: (n) A mystical land where 99% of all human productivity, motivation, and achievement is stored. (Unknown)

And guess what…this morning is the tomorrow we had yesterday. Start your morning out with intention, with fire, with purpose. In your morning writings make a list of all the things you've been putting off this month. We're halfway through June—but we still have half to go. The glass must always be half full, Mama. That's how we teach our loved ones to persevere, to dream, and to never, ever give up.

June 17

"It takes courage to grow up and become who you really are." ~E.E.
Cummings

I don't want to forget the hard work and fearlessness I had inside of me when I was a kid. As we navigate our children's childhoods, we can't forget how brave they are. How brave we were. We can't forget to give them the respect and grace they deserve as they face the enormous and enchanting task of growing up.

June 18

What we want. What we need. What we have. Sometimes I think we struggle with these three concepts. They say the devil lives in what we *want*. And if we think about it, we already have all we *need*. And true joy and happiness can be found in being grateful for what we already *have*. Remind yourself of this, Mama, as you go after your dreams. Follow your passion, ignite others to live their best, most creative selves today—but never forget to enjoy this beautiful journey as it unfolds.

June 19

I want to be a mom that my kids can relate to. It is a delicate balance between mom and friend that we have to maintain. Rules are essential. But recently I heard a saying that struck a chord within me.

...Rules without Reason equals Rebellion...

If we want our children to respect and understand the rules we set for them, we have to respect our kids enough to open up the dialogue. I try to not just say *"because I said so"*. I try to share with them the lessons I have learned along the way that make the rules easier to understand. Like I said, it's a ridiculously delicate balance. But no one ever said this parenting thing was easy.

June 20

Summer. A truly memorable time for a kid. Lake time. Beach time. Ice cream time. Family vacay time. Hiking time. Camping time. Canoe racing time. S'mores over a bonfire time. Fishing. Lemonade stands. Popsicle smiles. Barbecues and bubbles. Romances and first kisses. Catching lightning bugs and playing until the sun goes down. Get in the summertime groove today, Mama. Turn on The Beach Boys Pandora and make a bucket list for this summer. Make it memorable. Make it fun. Make it magic.

June 21

Summer Solstice—the longest day of the year. We get to feel the summer sunlight on our skin for more minutes on this day than any other day of the year. In ancient China, the solstice was a celebration of the Earth, femininity, and the "yin" forces. Native Americans danced to honor the sun. All over the world bonfires are lit and music is played to celebrate the life force and energy that our sun provides. Find a moment to express gratitude for the world. For this planet. For the incredible sunshine that relentlessly and faithfully shines for us every single day.

June 22

Sometimes, Mama…we just have to consciously let our worries go. It can be so hard, so heavy to carry fear and uncertainty around every day. Finances, children, work, love, life—the future can weigh me down. And for what? The future is not guaranteed, it's not even here yet. We have to live this day mindfully—conscious of every breath, every beat, every butterfly we get.

"The Lord will guide you always; he will satisfy your needs in a sun-scorched land and will strengthen your frame. You will be like a well-watered garden, like a spring whose waters never fail." ~Isaiah 58:11

June 23

Igniting Passion Journal Exercise
Spend a few moments today journaling about what makes you feel like a woman...

A woman is a powerful, mysterious, and enchanting being. So. What makes you feel like a woman? Are you taking some much needed time to act on the things that make you feel female? We have to remember the woman inside the mother, and that woman means something different to all of us. It helps to bring your core thoughts back to the page and write down the simple rituals or things that encourage your passionate side. And then go act on them, of course.

June 24

> *"While it served her in the past*
> *She refused to keep her magic*
> *contained, restrained,*
> *or detained any longer."*
> ~Rebecca Campbell, Rise Sister Rise

This is the time to realize that whatever you are desiring, whatever you wish to let loose on the world—it is no longer serving you to keep holding back. Now is the time to embrace your magic. And if it's hard to find the time or you feel guilty or selfish for something being just about you (this happens when we become mothers!), think about how you want your kids to grow up. What kind of role models do you wish them to look up to? Like it or not, Mama, you are one of their first role models. You are one of their very first examples of how well a life can be lived. Show them magic. Show them creativity. Show them that devoting their life to being true to themselves and following their passions is a joyful, inspiring, and fulfilling way to live.

June 25

What was the first thought you had when you woke up this morning? Keep a journal of this for one week and monitor what kind of soul food is in your mind. It is fascinating to see how our thoughts rule our day, our dreams, and our motivation. Make it a habit—no, make it a priority—to start your day with fabulous thoughts. Peaceful thoughts. Empowering thoughts. Loving thoughts. Every day will begin brighter and lighter...and that kind of passion is contagious.

June 26

"Some beautiful paths can't be discovered without getting lost." ~Erol Ozan,
Writer

Mom. That word can sometimes be synonymous with Control Freak. We work so hard to stay on schedule, follow the rules, do what's expected of us. Perhaps because the train would derail if we let go even a little bit. And kids thrive on rules, right? But maybe, just maybe, getting lost sometimes doesn't have to be the end of the world. So what if we have to ask for directions, or it takes a little longer to get where we're going. Some of my best memories growing up are of getting lost somewhere and the adventures that followed. So let's lighten up today, Mama. Let's loosen the reins. Let's get lost...and have some beautiful experiences that we could have never planned in all our wildest dreams.

June 27

"Care about what other people think and you will always be their prisoner."
~Lao Tzu

Don't let anything or anyone make you a prisoner. Mindfully and passionately working to live a creative life will free you forever, Mama. Teddy Roosevelt said, *"comparison is the thief of joy"*, and that quote is worth repeating to yourself until it sinks in. An authentic woman is striking. And stunning. And alluring. And free.

June 28

"I dream my painting, and then I paint my dream." ~Vincent van Gogh

A small reminder to reignite our creativity today. If you feel stuck and unsure of where to begin, start with your dreams. Then go out and make them your reality.

June 29

Open your eyes to a beautiful June day today. Every once in a while, it is lovely to stop and look around you. To take stock of all the dreams that have come true in your life. All the goals you've set for yourself that you have reached. All the milestones you've worked your tail off to achieve. And every single one of them you have accomplished yourself. You have made them happen. You have found the way to get it done. Action is the only antidote to fear and restlessness. It's the only answer to creating the life that you want. That is why it feels so great to do something risky. Something challenging. Something scary. However big or small, facing one small fear a day will awaken the warrior goddess inside of you. She is dying to come out and play, whenever you need her. And the more you remember how strong you have been and how many dreams you have already made your reality, the more courage you will have to keep going. To infinity and beyond, perhaps.

June 30

"A mother who radiates self-love and self-acceptance actually vaccinates her daughter against low self-esteem." ~Naomi Wolf, Author and Journalist

Wow. If there is one thing I have learned so far on my mamahood journey, it is that our children are so much more perceptive of our actions than we think. Already my two-year-old has learned the phrase "I can't"—and I hate it. I just want to take those two words from her little brain and replace them with "Yes", "Bring it on", "Let's do this!". She learns what she sees. So I guess it starts with me. With us, Mama. Let's teach our children self love by starting with loving ourselves first.

JULY

Feeding the Flame

July 1

It's travel time for so many of us this sunny and soul searching month of July! A mama friend told me to include some travel tips this month. She said never travel alone with a toddler and an infant. I said that's what wine is for. She said you don't have enough hands! I said sippy cups aren't just for water anymore.

It's the small things, Mama.

July 2

Let the heat of summer stoke the fire inside you today. Let the hope and childlike enjoyment of family and vacation and time well spent with your loved ones inspire you. And with that inspiration, you can make any dream you could possibly dream come true. The flame within that yearns for passion and creativity and success grows bigger with every bit of confidence you feed it. Hold onto that and be encouraged. The fires of summer are powerful. Let them empower you.

"Don't be pushed by your problems. Be led by your dreams." ~Ralph Waldo Emerson

July 3

This time of year is filled with family, friends, fun—and yes—fireworks. Make sure to slip away for even a moment and get some "you" time in. Don't get lost in the chaos and crazy. Your patience will wear down, and your soul will be thirsty for some rejuvenation. Perhaps it's an early morning sunrise session with nature on your patio. Or let the family run around after dinner, let the dishes wait a moment and slip into a candlelit bath or a quick meditation. Mama, don't be afraid to steal these much needed moments of solitude. These moments recharge and refill the heart, body, and mind.

July 4

Freedom. Liberty. Independence. Equality. Celebrate these words today. Feel the well of gratitude that we are raising our children in the land of the free. It's a gift and a right to respect and be grateful for.

"Oh Say does that Star Spangled Banner Yet Wave
O'er the Land of the Free
And the Home of the Brave."
~Francis Scott Key

July 5

The definition of perseverance can be seen every time you watch—or watched!—your bebe get up and try to walk. Do you remember that time? It's fascinating. It truly does not matter how many times they tumble, stumble, or fall flat on their face. They get right back up, giggling and excited to try again. If only *we* could live like that...

"Falling down is a part of life, getting back up is living." ~Brian Tracy, Author

July 6

"Live in each season as it passes; breathe the air, drink the drink, taste the fruit, and resign yourself to the influence of the Earth." ~Henry David Thoreau

Summer is some people's favorite season of the year. What is yours, Mama? It is not my favorite, so I struggle to live in the moment of the season, and not wish it away. I want to mindfully focus on this beautiful July day—enjoy the blazing sunshine, the cool lemonade, the peaches and plums that are always delightfully stacked at our Farmer's Market. What is special about July that we cannot get any other time of the year? That's what should be on our to-do list today.

July 7

It's simple. In order to keep feeding the flame of our creativity, we just need a few things. The small kindling, or habits—think positive affirmations, meditation, daily workout, morning journaling—to get the flame going. And then oxygen. It's all oxygen. Keep your inner flame going with the breath. Each breath leads to the next and the next and keeps you in the moment of every day. If you forget to breathe you will get bogged down by all the steps from here to where you want to be. But stay with the breath and you'll take each goal one beautiful moment at a time. Until before you know it, you have one awesome fire going.

July 8

"The world communicates subtly. Most people don't hear or see the signs because they're so wrapped up in their day-to-day lives." ~Doug Cooper, <u>Outside In</u>

A simple reminder to slow down and stay in touch with the vibrations in this world. This month is all about fun and vacation and kids at home all the time—ah! Tune into yourself for at least a moment every day. The morning can be the most powerful, before everyone wakes up. Breathe in and out…and listen. Listen to you heart, your mind, and your soul. The woman that glows inside will tell you secrets and stories you need to hear.

July 9

This month brings the heat, so we might as well jump on the bandwagon. Let's focus on feeding the flame of our creativity as we see summer arrive. A flame can burn red and orange which are the colors associated with our Sacral Chakra. This chakra is located in the pelvic region and is the center of our bliss and sensuality. It helps us make every day routine tasks much more interesting and pleasurable. Working on this chakra gently encourages personal and positive growth, which will lead to creative development and freedom in inspiration.

Try a simple chakra meditation today. Diffuse some orange and sandalwood essential oil if you have it. Sit quietly and breathe in and out. Focus your thoughts and breath on the pelvic sacral chakra. Imagine an orange soothing light glowing all around your hips and pelvis. Repeat these affirmations:

I am strong.
I love my temple of a body.
Every freckle, line, and hair is a sign of my inner goddess.

July 10

"Every time you are tempted to react in the same old way, ask if you want to be a prisoner of the past or a pioneer of the future." ~Deepak Chopra

I choose to be a pioneer of the future today. When I'm talking to my daughter, when I find myself feeling frustrated or burned out—I don't want to resort to old habits. I want to find patience in place of annoyance, grace in place of feeling sorry for myself, and laughter in place of aggravation. Most pioneers have to be innately optimistic people, right? Holding onto the faith that they will discover something grand and good—no matter how long it takes.

July 11

Everyone keeps saying *"These are the best years of your life. These are the best years of your life."* Over and over again I am reminded to hold onto these moments, cherish these cuddles, remember the kisses—because all too soon these babies grow up, and the sleepless nights, endless routine, and chaotic toddler years will end. But you know what, Mama? I remember my teenage years, my 20s—all the different phases in my life—and they were all pretty great in their own ways, too. Honestly every year should be the best year of our life. Every year should stand out in our memories for its challenges, its triumphs, its joys. Yes, enjoy these insane new momma years…but it is okay to be excited about what the future holds as well. The circle of life is powerful and romantic and nostalgic…so enjoy it all, Mama. Enjoy it all.

July 12

"Worrying does not take away tomorrow's troubles, it takes away today's peace."
~Unknown

Don't get too wrapped up in the big picture, Mama. The endgame of whatever project you are working on can become far away and overwhelming if all you focus on is the massive number of steps from here to there. Do not let how far you need to go stress you out to the point of giving up. Just take a breath…take a step back…and take one step at a time. What are the three things you need to do next? Do them. Then do the next three, and then the three after that. Big goals only get accomplished in little actions every day. Before you know it, you'll be amazed at how far you've come.

July 13

"With freedom, books, flowers, and the moon, who could not be happy?"
~Oscar Wilde

This is a trick to jumpstart your gratitude and happy meter, Mama. If you are feeling a bit empty, come back to the four things that you know make you happy. When the world is conspiring to bring us down, we have to fight back with whatever we can. So what are those four things?

There's your antidote for a blah day. And whatever that happiness tool is, do not feel guilty when you have to reach into your bag and use it. A yoga class, a glass of lovely rosé, a movie date (even if it's on your couch), a solitary walk on the beach...the tools are out there and endless. We are always talking about positive redirection with our children—why not try it for ourselves every now and then?

July 14

Sky above me,
Earth below me,
Fire within me.
~Unknown

These three things are true. Know this in the core of your being and live this mantra today. There is endless possibility in front of you if you can let your soul fly, stay grounded, and burn all at once.

July 15

"Sometimes your only available transportation is a leap of faith." ~Margaret Shepherd, Calligrapher, Author

I am so drawn to this quote right now. The perfect motivation for halfway through the seventh month of the year. Life is filled with bumps and bruises, and it is all about how we learn to navigate and view these bruises that make us the women we want to be. Does a challenge depress you? Fire you up? I wish we were always battle ready—thick skinned and sword drawn. But we're not. We have weak spots and insecurities and weary days sometimes. We just cannot wallow in those insecurities. Let them flow through you, and then get on to the gettin' on. Take a leap. Have faith that you will land somewhere wonderful.

July 16

Wherever you are right now, get on the floor and stretch. Do cobbler's pose—sit with the soles of your feet pressed together and lean forward—to release tension in your hips. Thread your fingers behind your back and find space in those shoulders that carry so much every day. Find a scarf, lie on your back and hook the scarf over the ball of one foot. Pull gently back as you straighten your leg, and feel the burn in your hamstrings. And breathe. Always breathe. We have to keep the energy moving fluidly throughout our bodies, Mama. You'll feel 10 pounds lighter and 10 inches taller after you do some simple stretching every so often in your day. If the energy gets stuck, our creativity and inspiration will get stuck as well. Keep it moving. Keep it flowing…keep it seeking.

July 17

"There are some things you learn best in calm, and some in storm" ~Willa Cather, Author

I must remind myself that there is a season for everything. I may prefer to learn in the calm, but I have been through enough storms to know that the major growth happens there. And so I will tell myself this when I have to watch my children go through a storm as well. They are learning. They are making mistakes. They are growing. They are living.

July 18

Summer is filled with family and vacation and adventure...as well as a total disregard for routine and rules. This is delicious and delightful at the time, but it wreaks havoc on re-entry to the real world when you come back. Whether it's the time change, losing the five pounds you may or may not have gained (mmmmm desserts...and mai tais...and pancakes...), or just tackling the kids on your own again— take a minute before the day starts to center yourself, Mama. We cannot reach our goals and center our kids without centering ourselves first. Turn on some Parisian cafe music and savor that cup of coffee, tea, or smoothie. And breathe. Breathe in this truly magnificent life. Then greet that pitter patter (or stampede) of feet with a grin on your face that can take over the world.

July 19

Before many yoga sessions, you set an intention for your practice. A mantra or idea or word you want to breathe in and meditate on for that short span of time. But this morning, I'd like to set an intention for the short span of 12-14 hours that I am awake. So. Here goes. *Today is the first day of the rest of my life. I will live this day with passion and humor. I will live this day with passion and humor. I will live this day with passion and humor. I will live this day...*

What is your intention for this day, Mama? See it. Set it. Live it.

July 20

It is National Moon Day. The moon fascinates me. It always has. Do you feel that mysterious ancient pull to the moon that so many women do? Maybe it's the ever changing shape of it that inspires me to believe that change is a good thing. Our cups empty and overflow and refill—and that is ok. That is life. That is motherhood. Maybe it's the luminous silver to pewter to gold color of it that sets my creative soul on fire and causes dreams to awaken to reality. It helps calm my overworked mama brain to just take a deep breath, step outside, and look at the moon. If that moon can handle change as much as she does, surely we all can too. Gracefully...and steadfast.

July 21

"The body registers thought as much as it registers action." ~Elena Brower, Yoga Instructor

What are you struggling with right now, Mama? Where is the energy stuck? Is it kids? Finding yourself amidst the overwhelming title of "mom"? Perhaps you are navigating a new pregnancy while raising the babes you already have. Or maybe you feel you don't have enough time in the day to get all the tasks and to-do lists checked off. In order to take on our struggles, and learn to either let them go or live with them, we have to be incredibly mindful of our thoughts. It doesn't matter how much yoga or running or barre method or spa trips we participate in, your body responds equally to both action and thought. Thought. Stay protective of the thoughts you allow to take root. Spin the negative into positive as much as you can. Find the gratitude—and find peace.

July 22

Psychologytoday.com states seven scientifically proven benefits to giving an attitude of gratitude a try:

Gratitude opens the door to more relationships.
Gratitude improves physical health.
Gratitude improves psychological health.
Gratitude enhances empathy and reduces aggression.
Grateful people sleep better.
Gratitude improves self-esteem.
Gratitude increases mental strength.

It is simple. A grateful heart opens doors, improves life, lifts your self esteem, opens your mind—and most importantly, Mama?—it helps you sleep more. Mic drop.

July 23

"If only our eyes saw souls instead of bodies, how very different our ideals of beauty would be." ~Unknown

Can we teach our little ones to see souls today? To recognize service and respect as beautiful instead of clothes and hairstyles? We—you and I, Mama—have to be the ones to teach them this incredibly crucial difference. You know those people, the ones who see beauty in the soul instead of the skin. They are the most inspiring, peaceful, magnetic people in the world. It is up to us to nurture more of that on this complicated and delicious planet. It's up to us first to decide what beautiful is. And it is up to us to teach what beautiful is to our children.

July 24

I am an introverted extrovert. What are you? How do you recharge your batteries? Through other people? Or do you need solitude, a good book, or a binge session on Netflix to fill up the reserve? My husband finds more energy from being around people, social environments, lots of noise and busyness. I enjoy being social—but it drains me. I need time to myself to keep my motivation, my inspiration, and my sanity. It took us a long time to figure out this dichotomy, but once we did, it changed our whole dynamic for the good. Because we finally understood and accepted each other's "recharging" methods. I encourage you to look inside yourself, talk to the people who are most important to you and see what kind of people you all are. We have to learn how to communicate our needs to each other—especially when most of our days are filled with giving, giving, giving...

July 25

"Listen to the sounds of the waves within you." ~Rumi

We are in the seventh month of the year. More than halfway to next year. Before you know it, we'll be drinking pumpkin spice lattes and taking adorable pumpkin patch pictures with our little ones. But whatever heat wave you are in—don't wish these last months of summer away. Tap into yourself, your soul. Today I challenge you to not let the outside world creep in, and find time to meditate, journal, or take a yoga class online. Refocus your intentions for this year—if only to make sure you are listening to what your heart and inner flame are telling you.

"Listen to...the waves within you..." Our intentions, our dreams ebb and flow. So let them...and listen.

July 26

"I would like to be known as an intelligent woman, a courageous woman, a loving woman. A woman who teaches by being." ~Maya Angelou

Yes. Yes. Yes. Yes. *A woman who teaches by being.* We must live with courage, love, and intelligence every single day. We must stay authentic in our journey through motherhood, so we can encourage those around us to find their own true selves. How much more interesting would we all be if we weren't trying to be like everyone else all the time?

July 27

Encourage your inner flame to glow today. If you need some help getting started, try the yogic Breath of Fire technique. Close your eyes and start to exhale in short, fast bursts through your nose. The inhale happens naturally so focus on the exhale. Find a fast and powerful rhythm from your diaphragm. and keep going for one to three minutes. Practicing this breath for a short time every day will lead you to all kinds of energy shifts and can even lead to getting over addictions. But most importantly, it will stimulate your inner pilot light and get that creativity flowing!

July 28

"If we have no peace it is because we have forgotten we belong to each other."
~Mother Teresa

When we need to find calm, when we need to find patience, when we need to hold our babies instead of yell—again–I come back to this quote. We belong to each other. That's the message I want to give my children. We are a family, we are all in this together, we belong to each other. So we must love, cherish, laugh, and respect. Take a deep breath, Mama, and remember who you belong to.

July 29

"Don't worry about trying to find your life's purpose. Instead, start by acting on the small things that excite you each day. These are the threads that will connect you to your path, passion, and purpose in life." ~Ruben Chavez

Now is as good a time as any to look at our goals and aspirations. The summer is filled with frenzy and family—it is easy to lose sight of your inner pilot light. Before you know it, you have slipped into that rut of routine that will burn you out fast. If you need help finding that flame again, come back to this quote. Figure out the small things that make your heart beat faster...and start following that fascinating path.

July 30

Keep encouraging the light today. There is no room for comparison, boredom, or frustration inside your world. Jealousy is an ugly companion to walk around life with—so try to view it as a wake up call instead. A cold hard truth indicator. Every person, thing, or life that you are jealous of is an opportunity to discover new dreams and goals to set for yourself. There is room for everyone to live creatively in this abundant world. There is space for all dreams to come true. Don't let jealousy hold you back from the woman you want to be. Instead run joyfully in the direction of the light.

July 31

"This is a wonderful day. I've never seen this one before." ~Maya Angelou

Enjoy this sweet last lovely day of July. Every sun kissed, sand covered, grass stained, firefly moment of it. You've never been here before.

AUGUST

Back to Basics

The Daily Soul Sessions For Every Mama

August 1

Today is National Girlfriends Day. Uh—Heck. Yes. This is the day to celebrate your tribe, Mama. This is the day to plan a brunch with the women that encourage you, motivate you, and love you. A goddess tribe of women that you have worked hard to surround yourself with. No room for judgement or toxic people in this group! And that is something to celebrate. #GNO here we come!

August 2

"So come with me where dreams are born, and time is never planned. Just think of happy things, and your heart will fly on wings...forever." ~Betty Comden and Adolf Green for Peter Pan

My thoughts are my reality. Your thoughts are your reality. What reality do you want to manifest on this day? We live in a challenging time to raise dreamers and doers. I choose to lead by example—let grace, fun, and forgiveness guide my day. I refuse to let a challenging toddler, a bump in the road to success, or the blistering heat be my compass. Not today. Not today.

August 3

I stumbled across an anonymous quote today:

"...August is like the Sunday of Summer..."

I felt waves of nostalgia and romance and anticipation. We'd better enjoy this month to its sticky sweet fullest. August is the hazy burn of a sunset, it's the quiet peace before a new work week begins. It's the bittersweet end of summer camp or a truly magical vacation. August is a great month. And it's all ahead of us right now.

August 4

August: *Respected and impressive. (Google.com)*

I did not know the definition of that word. August. It inspires admiration and celebration. All qualities I could channel a little more of today. Celebrate this day for no other reason than you're alive and smiling and loved.

August 5

Everyone always says to be careful who our children surround themselves with. You know, stranger danger and all that—and leading up to who they choose as their friends in school. But it is equally as important to surround ourselves very mindfully as well. The little ones around us are curious sponges. And so are we, come to think of it. Garbage in, garbage out my Mama always used to say, and it makes a lot of sense. August is all about getting back to the basics and remembering our core values, and most of the time the heart of those values is simple. Toxic people and habits have no room in the confident and illuminated worlds we are building. And it feels so darn good to leave that poison behind.

Journal Exercise
Spend a few minutes today writing down some unhealthy habits or people that you are dealing with in your life right now. How do they make you feel? How would you feel if they didn't affect you or control your emotions the way they do? What steps or affirmations can you take in the moment to start to let that negativity simply pass through your heart and keep going. Don't let this negativity pool inside of you. Freeing up that space makes room for the good and inspiring that is longing to be there instead.

August 6

Spend some time in Nature today. Smell the flowers. Feel the sunshine on your skin. Take a walk down a winding road and find all the fascinating, twisting, towering trees along the way. Look at those trees as a metaphor for the life you want to live. A tree's branches, leaves, colors are what we present to the world. The way that tree sways or stands firm no matter the storm can inspire us. However, it wouldn't be that tree without doing the work deep down. In its roots. The roots are actually the most important part of who and what that tree is.

So let's start there. Deep down. A root provides the nourishment, the life force. What nourishes you, what lights your inner pilot light? What makes you feel grounded and secure in your life? You have to seek that out, find it, nurture it, and then search for more.

August 7

Getting back to the basics of what we really need and want in this life can be a tough process. It involves a lot of letting go of bad habits, clearing clutter, and encouraging self-assessment. But it is completely essential if you want to live a freer, more inspired life. The baggage of the past and regrets have no place in our roles as women and mothers right now. So. Find a way to move on from the parts of you that hurt or hold you back. Move on from your mistakes. It's ok to move on. Say that to yourself one hundred times—until you believe it. It is ok to move on.

"Perhaps in the breaking, we can find the healing we long for." ~Jay Wolf,
Hope Heals

August 8

Happiness happens. Believe it. They even dedicated a whole day to it. It's today. Happiness is a state of mind, and you cannot just wait for it to happen to you. You must go out and grasp it. And create it. And hold steadfast to it. And seek it out. Decide to be happy. Decide to do the things that make you smile. Decide to spend time with the people that inspire you. Decide to learn about things that fascinate you. Decide to teach your kids the lessons that are important to you. This is how you make happiness happen.

August 9

We are deep in the days of summer. The heat seems to be settling in for a sweltering, suffocating stay. Don't let the temperature send your mood into a tailspin. Blissful fall is just a few weeks away. The seasons alone teach us how temperamental and evolving our lives are. This day will lead to the next, thank goodness, so train your mind to never let the bad get you down for too long. New days and new opportunities are always just around the corner.

"A mind set in its ways is wasted. Don't do it." ~Eric Schmidt, executive chairman, Google.

August 10

There are four babies born every second. Every second. With 80 million mamas in the US alone it is incredible that we ever feel isolated in this motherhood journey (soundvision.com). And yet...we do. Being a mom can be so lonely sometimes—and the key to happiness is to learn to fight that feeling. To seek out other moms, to keep searching and nurturing the tribe that can keep us going when we are feeling uninspired. So. Start a book—ehem wine—club with your girlfriends. Plan a picnic with the kids and other moms. Simply start an email chain with your favorite ladies, and let them all know how much you appreciate them. We are not alone in this. We were not meant to be alone in this. And you can find faith in that.

August 11

Dear Self,
Please continue to learn. Explore all new things and really enjoy your youth. Exercise and eat right. Play, laugh, dance, love, sing. Keep learning. Read. Dream. Inspire! Make the conscious choice to be inspiring. Collect rocks and plant a garden, make a star chart, meditate, pray daily, practice yoga, and feed your soul. Ok? Ok. Good talk.

August 12

This month we work on getting back to the basics in our lives by remembering what is truly important, and by clearing out the clutter so we can make room for creativity and innovation. A great way to start getting back to the basics is to balance your root chakra. It is the first energy point at the base of your spine, and it represents your physical being, your most basic needs. Safety, survival, instinct. Focus on the color red today, surround yourself in nature, sit on the ground, brush your teeth, get a pedicure—seriously!—all these things will help you to feel grounded and bring you back into your physical self. Diffuse frankincense and clove essential oils if you have them, and use these affirmations today:

I am safe.
I have all that I need.
I trust myself.
I love this life.

August 13

"The future depends on what we do in the present." ~Mahatma Gandhi

Maybe you're tired. Maybe it's been a tough week. But every day and every moment lead us to the next. So make this day, this moment a good one…it'll only take you to even better moments ahead. Change this moment for the better. Right now. All you have to do is decide, and like magic, the future is brighter already.

August 14

Do you know what is amazing, Mama? Our happiest days are yet to come. It's true. My husband says that to me all the time, and it brings such a sense of peace, joy, and anticipation. New adventures, new kids, new surprises, new...everything. Who knows what is waiting down the road...

...and we get to be a part of dreaming, scheming, and creating that happiness.

August 15

Today is Relaxation Day. *Relaxation is the state of being free from tension and anxiety (Google.com).* So in honor of this wonderful day, take some time for yourself. What is the one thing you love to do to relax? Self care helps keep us sane in these foggy parent years. It is truly amazing how even one hour to yourself can turn your whole day around. Your mind creates space to breathe and come back to itself. And then you are more open and loving and excited to spend time with those adorable tornadoes—um—I mean toddlers...

August 16

Regular People: *Sorry I'm late! Traffic was nuts.*

Moms: *Sorry I'm late. My daughter's sweater was too sweater-y, and the baby ate a band-Aid.*

It's Tell A Joke Day. HA. *(facebook.com/Shakespearesmom)*

August 17

"To live a creative life, we must lose our fear of being wrong." ~Joseph Chilton Pearce

What if…what it…what if…Is that thought circling in your brain these days? New school year, fall so close we can taste the pumpkin spice, football just around the corner. It's easy to dream and come up with "what ifs" this time of year. The end of that sentence is your creativity trying so hard to break free. What if…I started that gardening class. What if…I launched my own business. What if…we finally planned that trip to Italy. What if…it all came true?

Your kids are starting a new year. So why don't you as well? What if…What if…What if…

August 18

Food for thought: France recently passed a law that gives citizens the "right to disconnect" after work hours. The French people were convinced that this digital age was severely limiting the time we need to connect with other human beings as opposed to our work emails. Fascinating, right? Instead of feeling obligated to stay in touch every hour of every day with work, they now have the right to turn off those phones and dive into what really matters. Conversation, a good meal, time well spent, hobbies, friends...life. Vive La France!

August 19

"Your instincts, your personal intuition always whispers. It never shouts. Listen to the whisper..." ~Steven Spielberg

Listen. We constantly tell our kids to listen. Listen. Listen. But do we ever follow our own advice? Our real, raw, and deep dreams are quiet. They whisper in our ear. If we don't slow down and find the silence, we will never be able to hear them through the madness and the chaos. So let's listen today. Let's see what the world has to tell us. Let's see what our hearts have to tell us.

August 20

The whirl of schedules and normal life may start to catch you off guard as the hazy magic of summer gets ruthlessly stripped away. Take some time today to set goals for yourself and your family as everyone becomes busy, busy, busy. Build back in mindful time with your kids at the beginning and end of each day—breakfast together, family dinners—whatever that looks like for you. Those sweet little ones still need their Mama...more than ever when life gets crazy.

August 21

Wake up, Mama. Wake up. From the moment you open your eyes to the moment you close them—let's notice the little things today. The little details that make our day into something we love, cherish, and work hard for. Say *"I love my..."* over and over to yourself as you start to appreciate the tiny things that are working together in your life.

I love my...strong husband snoring beside me—he is such a positive soul.
I love my...stone bedroom floor as it meets the worn wood in the hallway.
I love my...coffee machine—definition of efficient.
I love my...quiet house and beautiful sleeping babe that give me a blessed moment to start my day.

What do you love? Look for it in this day. It's there—in all its quiet and fierce and steadfast beauty.

August 22

Back to school, back to basics this week. Let's have a solid seven days of good old-fashioned reboot.

Day One...Let Go
Practice makes perfect so we need to practice the art of letting go. Forgive yourself for whatever you need to right now. This second. Breathe in the judgement you put on yourself. Breathe in the food choices you are regretting from the weekend. Breathe in the words or thoughts you unwillingly had toward your husband, your kids. Breathe in the dirty kitchen, the unwashed laundry. Then exhale. And send those thoughts as far away as you can. Let them go.

Now breathe in this beautiful, messy, adventurous, unique, and magical life that is all yours. It's all yours. So love it. And go live it.

August 23

Day Two...Set Goals
Back to basics, Mama. Take 15 minutes today—whenever you can sneak in a small break for yourself—and write down your goals. Start by writing down your Perfect Day. This day is in the future—what does it look like to you? Where do you live? What does your house look like? Husband, kids, job, joy. Be specific and dream big as you do this. Make it so real you can taste and smell that life. Feel the excitement that setting goals brings. Getting back to the basics means reminding yourself of what you want for your family, for yourself, all the while figuring out what is missing so we can fill our lives up all the way to the brim.

"Setting goals is the first step in turning the invisible into the visible." ~Tony Robbins

August 24

Day Three...Get Strong

Getting back to the basics in our body is just as important as in our soul. It takes 21 days to break a habit. 21 days. And in these 21 days, we can start to form better habits. What kind of body cleanse can you make a part of your life, starting today? Go to yogaglo.com and choose a class or meditation. Start a juice cleanse or get rid of processed foods in your diet. Commit to 50 push-ups, 100 sit-ups, and 10 minutes of stretching a day. Then decide to continue these new habits. Just see how you feel as days begin to pass. Keep a journal so you can go back and read for yourself how much your body is thanking you. Choose some sort of basic reboot that is dedicated to the strong, feminine, goddess, warrior body that has carried you and your babes this far in life. Honor that body. Cherish that body. And rock that body today.

August 25

Day Four...Be Unique

"You are allowed to be both a masterpiece and a work in progress, simultaneously." ~Sophia Bush

Everything about you is unique. Your kids, your home, your husband...your dreams. Embrace that uniqueness. Stop trying to fit into any kind of mold or group or category and be blessedly free. Be quirky. Be you. Remember yourself as a child—before the expectations, before the rules you put on yourself. Come back to that person. Come back to that fabulous independent heart. And then accept that you are a masterpiece that is just getting better...

With...every...passing...heartbeat.

August 26

Day Five...Set Your Foundation

Basic: *Forming   an   essential   foundation   or   starting   point. (Oxforddictionaries.com)*

...An essential foundation. We cannot instill confidence, strength, or passion in our children if we haven't worked on ourselves first. Life comes along and changes us, teaches us, enlightens us. But in order to be unmoved by the things that do not bring us joy and inspiration, we have to work on our foundation. What is elementally us—who did we want to be when we grew up—and are we anything like that person now?

Get to your yoga mat, do some short meditations or journaling, take some time to be by yourself so you can hear your own heartbeat. Come back to your basic soul and remember how powerful that woman is. Before mom, before sister, before wife, before friend...you were just you. Unique and lovely and intriguing...

...You.

August 27

Day Six...Find Gratitude

"In order to love who you are, you cannot hate the experiences that shaped you."
~Andrea Dykstraf

Every blessing, heartache, or challenge has made you the woman you are. Don't waste one second on hate. Find the gratitude. Search for it as desperately as one searches for a soulmate. Do not let regret rule your day. Because one day soon you will be navigating these waters with your daughter or son. And we must teach those precious souls strength, courage, and endless optimism.

August 28

Day Seven...Be Creative

Choose your own back to basics theme today. The options are endless...

Make Green Smoothies
Do Sun Salutations
Fix a big green salad for dinner
Drink hot water with lemon
Watch a feel good Fall movie
Wash bed sheets
Light candles all throughout the house

A full week of recharging and centering is so important, so therapeutic, and so soul satisfying.

August 29

> *"Summer will end soon enough, and childhood as well."* ~George R.R. Martin, A Game of Thrones

Enjoy the sweetness of your babe's laughter. Savor the innocence of their endless questions. Be grateful for the lessons you get to pass on. Soak in the memories that a summer day holds. When life gets hard, when routine gets depressing, when days seem long...

...just remember it'll be over before we know it. So make memories. Make memories. Make memories.

August 30

Start this morning or recharge your afternoon with a mantra. Sit comfortably somewhere, close your eyes, keep your palms open and receiving. Steady your breath. On the inhale think *I am connected.* On the exhale think *We are powerful.* Repeat this over and over as you touch the ground, your heart, hold your hands out to the sky. Kathryn Budig, yoga teacher and all around rockstar, keeps this up for a solid five minutes.

It is invigorating to connect with the silence and energy that flows around us. It reminds us that the world is bigger than our house, our kitchen, our problems. When we are connected to this bigger picture we can start again with humility, gratitude, and light.

August 31

"If you don't go after what you want, you'll never have it. If you don't ask, the answer is always no. If you don't step forward, you're always in the same place."
~Nora Roberts, Author

Are you seeing the theme here? If nothing ever changes, then nothing ever changes. The time is now to be fearless in pursuing the woman and mother you want to be. Every good thing that has ever happened to me came from a scary, new, or unknown leap of faith. What do you have to lose?

SEPTEMBER

Embracing Change

September 1

Hello September. The ninth month of the year. The element of this month is the *EARTH*, and the stone is the Sapphire. Sapphires represent intuition and clarity of thought. This month will bring us a much anticipated season: Autumn. We have a few weeks yet until we fall into fall—so let's enjoy our Indian Summer while we can. This seriously stunning month is bursting with color, with fire, with hints of the harshness yet to come. It's as if the whole earth is begging to be noticed before it sheds its leaves and goes into hibernation. Breathe in September, Mama. It is yours for the living.

September 2

Let this new month drench you with determination today.

"Create the highest, grandest vision possible for your life, because you become what you believe." ~Oprah Winfrey

Do not give up on yourself. On your dreams. Keeping the fire stoked and your passions awakened is hard in the midst of motherhood. Your self melts into the endless tasks of to-do lists, and your energy is hard to find when you finally have a moment to yourself. But take courage, lady. There are mamas out there who find the spark. Who dig deep for the energy. You can do it, too. And the payoff is priceless. And all that work on yourself is as seductive and rewarding as seeing your children succeed. You can have both. So go get it.

September 3

If nothing ever changes, then nothing ever changes. I love this mantra. I repeat this thought whenever I feel fear or resistance of the future. You know the feeling. Procrastination, indecisiveness, laziness, smallness. These are signs of fear getting the best of you. Whether it's a date with sleep training, potty training, personal training, or something else you need to do that you're putting off— just remember that change is the most hopeful thing in this world. The possibility of change is what gets you to the life you want for yourself. For your family. For the world.

September 4

Change is in the air. Even if the leaves aren't yet turning from green to gold, or the mornings aren't quite cool enough for a crackling fire by your hearth, the subtle slide from summer to fall is coming. This is one change that the majority of people look forward to it seems. Everyone loves fall, so it's easy to embrace this change in our lives. Think about that for a moment. If only we could view all types of change with this optimism—this sense of childlike anticipation. It would make change not so scary…not so unknown. We'd greet it like an old friend—just waiting to sit down, share stories, and accept change into our lives. Gracefully. Peacefully. Happily.

September 5

The weather here has been cooperating with the *"I'm so excited for Fall, I can hardly stand it"* vibes I'm putting out lately. Cloudy and cool in the mornings with the sun burning through in the afternoon. Behind that sunshine there is a hint of the Season that is nipping at Summer's heels. This morning, however, I find myself wanting to look back for a moment. I always spend so much time looking ahead—next week, next month, next project, next play date. Do you ever spend some precious time remembering? Whip out your photos on the iPhone, set your apple TV to "collage" and just go through the summer memories you've made with your family the past three months. It is part of life, part of the process of staying mindful to be grateful for the gifts and adventures you've been given. There are a summers worth of smiles and laughter that are worth remembering, Mama...

September 6

Readers are leaders, isn't that the saying? I am a book lover, I have been all my life. I so hope I have passed on my love for stories and books to my daughter. There is truly nothing like the adventure that a novel can take you on, and the lessons a book whispers to you stay with you forever. I read to learn. How can we teach our children about love, life, and the great big world around us if we are not learning right alongside them? It's National Read a Book Day, so open a dusty cover and go on an adventure today. Romance, history, science fiction, mystery—all these worlds are just waiting for us.

September 7

Let the coming change in seasons remind you how cyclical this life is. One day our children will grow up and live a life that is all their own. And all we can do is try to prepare them for that day. My control freak side comes out more than ever since I became a Mama. I guess we are so consumed with keeping our babies safe and protected, it can be hard to let go of that control. But we have to. We have to practice a little bit, every day, as we raise these magnificent humans, to let go. It'll make them—and us—so much stronger in the end.

September 8

It never fails. At some point, you will feel like a failure as a mom. Your sweet little one will bite a kid at preschool, or you'll forget to pack them lunch, or they aren't potty trained as soon as you want them to be. Or it could be for a million other reasons...all just as frustrating to deal with as the next. These days come and go. When they hit me like a ton of bricks, I have to sit down by myself and take a few deep breaths. Then ask myself honestly—have I done all I can to fix, prevent, educate my child on this situation?

The times we feel like we haven't done the right thing are hard to let go of—but the only way to move on is to start fresh from that moment forward. Because we are doing enough. We are enough. Parenting is a constant learning process and a long journey for you and your kid, and none of us are experts yet. Forgive your children. They are beginners at this whole "life" thing. And forgive yourself. You are still new at this whole "parenting" thing. But love and laughter can go a long, long way to fixing almost anything.

September 9

"She wasn't doing a thing that I could see, except standing there leaning on the balcony railing, holding the universe together." ~J. D. Salinger, "A Girl I Knew"

This quote hit me hard today. As mothers, we hold our small slices of the universe together every day. The goal is to hold it together with grace and compassion. And to never be afraid to ask for help when we need it.

September 10

"Ten years from now, make sure you can say that you chose your life. You didn't settle for it." ~Mandy Hale

Choose your day. Choose your attitude. Choose your path. Choose your reactions. Choose your effort. Choose your friends. Choose your love. Choose your focus.

It starts now. Choose.

September 11

On this day, the best thing we can do is breathe, give, think, send, follow, and show love. Love is the answer to hurt. Love is the weapon to combat fear. Love is stronger than hate. Love can change the world. And love will ease your soul. Breathe love today. The world needs it.

September 12

Seasons help us to embrace change. They force us to accept a power and will stronger than ourselves, and to respect the circle and cycle of life. These tools of accepting change will help us to accept and ride the waves of motherhood as well. Everything is a phase. All stages are temporary. And man does the time go fast in the end. Filter this into your affirmations when you find yourself in a particularly challenging phase, Mama.

This too shall pass.
Nothing lasts forever.
The cycle of life is always evolving.
My kid will not throw tantrums forever.
When in doubt, pour a glass of wine.

See? You'll be feeling better in no time.

September 13

Phase: a distinct period or stage in a process of change or forming part of something's development. (Google.com)

I train myself to look at change as a good and necessary part of life, not a scary one. Change is the only way we get better, the only way dreams come true. So whatever phase you are in right now—happy, challenging, lucky, or exhausting—let's just remind ourselves that it is a distinct period. And it is all part of this process of change, this process of life, to get us where we are going. So either be grateful for this phase or look at it with hope for the phase that's coming after. Because something is coming. Light and love and magic and laughter. It's always coming. Can't you feel it?

September 14

Dear mothers, grand and great, first timers and seasoned birthers, and bright mama's to be...

We have a job to do. We are the life givers, entrusted with the extraordinary gift of creating life, and then guiding it. We must come together and drop a new pebble in the lake of humanity, and let the ripples of compassion, of kindness, of protection, of peace spread. It is our responsibility to nurture our children and those around us...to teach them and show them that life is precious and equal. We literally were given the gift and the power to create a new world. It starts with us, mamas...it starts with love.

September 15

"Dripping water hollows out stone, not through force but through persistence."
~Ovid

Set this quote on repeat in your head on the days your will is wavering. What part of your life needs this reminder? In parenting...in work...in determination...stay steady as the sun and consistent as the sunrise...you will get where you are going. You will.

September 16

Journal Exercise
Let's talk about Freedom.

What does it mean to you? We all want freedom in our lives, but it can look very different for different people. We have to become so clear, so confident in what that freedom looks like to us. In your journaling today, start with the phrase

I have freedom in...

Then finish that sentence in whatever way and however many times you can. *Freedom in work. Freedom in time. Freedom in vacation. Freedom in hours spent at the office...*

What does freedom look like to you?

September 17

As women we are emotional, connected, empowered beings. I love that the little things excite us. I love that pumpkin spice lattes and the coming of fall can recharge and revive us in a way that our husbands never quite grasp. Inspiration truly starts with you, Mama, and it always will. Without your heart, your laughter, your sense of magic, another day turns into just that—another day. So. How can we make this day one for the books? Because Thank God and Namaste—you get another day to breathe in this sassy, unpredictable, limitless life.

September 18

"Life has a way of testing a person's will, either by having nothing happen at all or by having everything happen at once." ~Paulo Coelho

There is something about September. The lazy days of summer and vacation are O-V-E-R, and the chaos and insanity of the school year has begun. Wow. Take a breath and dive straight into the fun, because it's happening whether you're ready or not. Sometimes the busyness helps to focus me more…let's go with that attitude today. Let your inner organized soul shine right now, Mama. Who doesn't love a brand new day planner anyway?

September 19

Being a creative person day in and day out can be challenging as mothers. Focusing on yourself, your desires, your strengths is a foreign feeling for us as we get swept away in our family's needs every day. But practicing mindful love toward ourselves for a moment now and then is essential to keep your creativity, spontaneity and sanity alive and well. What makes you unique from other mothers you know?

Journal about that today. Take a few well deserved minutes to send love and gratitude to yourself. Acknowledge the things that make you fabulous. We are all made differently, thank goodness!

I think moms are the most creative beings of all. We just have to find the courage and the commitment to keep pursuing it. And that is a challenging way to live—but a beautiful one.

September 20

There are 102 days left in this year. 102. What could we possibly do with 102 days? Five of my favorite holidays are packed into this last part of the year—first day of fall, Halloween, Thanksgiving, Christmas, and New Years. Phew. No wonder we all love this time of year. So much to look forward to and celebrate. It's definitely time to bring out the fall decorations, don't you think?

September 21

Today is World Gratitude Day. For 24 hours we have no excuse not to be mindfully overflowing with thanksgiving. Gratitude will sustain and strengthen you in the hard times, and inspire and enchant you in the good. What is true in the light is also true in the dark, so find a way to be hopeful in all parts of this day. Good, bad—dark, light—funny, serious. It is all a part of your journey today. So be grateful for it.

September 22

Dear Diary,

Today is the first day of fall and I love everything about you…

Pumpkin Patches
Falling Leaves
Halloween
Boots, Scarves, and Hats
Apple cider
Football
Practical Magic
Pumpkin Spice Lattes

Feel free to add to the list…

September 23

Sometimes the chaos in life randomly slows down and we find ourselves with a little free time. Isn't it ridiculous how fast boredom sets in? Or even worse—we seem to have forgotten how to enjoy the stillness. If the day isn't jam packed from sun up to sundown, we feel like we aren't doing enough. Being enough. But sometimes Mama, it is enough to just be. To enjoy the silence. To accept and be grateful for the pauses in a hectic life. If you find yourself in the midst of one of these pauses...pull your little one close, snuggle and watch a movie, read a book, have a cup of tea...and breathe.

September 24

"Don't Wait to Celebrate..." ~Katherine Wolf, <u>Hope Heals</u>

The only day we are promised is this day. Right now. Drink that champagne, use the good china, light the expensive candles...don't wait to celebrate, Mama. That is true mindfulness.

September 25

I am reading a wonderful book called <u>Hope Heals</u>, by Katherine and Jay Wolf. It is a story of triumph, devastation, love, and above all—hope. Book club this book next month, Mama, you won't regret it. It led me to thinking about my love story. And all of my friend's love stories. Each of our stories are totally unique and special to the other. It brought me to a sense of wonder and inspiration that out of all the roads, all the detours, all the decisions and mistakes and what ifs—somehow the path was laid specifically to bring two people together. Take a moment today to think about your path. Whether it's the path to your love or the path that led you to having that precious babe, think about it today. Be thankful that we get to experience such love. It is life changing.

September 26

So this is my soul's journey. This growth period. This time where I must learn the art of sacrifice. Of being happy for others living their lives freely, while gracefully accepting the small limitations in mine. If I want to be this compassionate, inspiring, positive force then I *MUST* live it. I must be it. And most importantly, I must believe it. It's all about the power of the mind…the mind can completely overpower the soul if we let it. Whether that's in negativity or positivity—the choice is up to me. So once again—a daily choice—I choose positivity. I choose to believe in my journey.

September 27

"'Dear God,' she prayed, 'let me be something every minute of every hour of my life.'" ~Betty Smith, <u>A Tree Grows in Brooklyn</u>

What is it today? Is it beauty? Working out? Dominating in the kitchen? Entertaining your children? A promotion at work? We all strive to excel in every moment of every day, but perhaps that is too far reaching. Perhaps that is simply too heavy for one single day. Let's lighten up, shall we? Instead of mastering it all right now, let's focus on one thing. Be a dreamer today—be a dreamer for our children. Get them in the kitchen, sit down and do an art project. Let's excel at parenthood today. The rest can wait for tomorrow.

September 28

Sometimes I wake up in the morning and my energy feels stuck. Do you ever feel this way? The creativity, positivity, and excitement for the new day is elusive. I feel sluggish instead of spiritual, heavy instead of hopeful. We don't have to follow that path though.

Try this when you feel that rut coming on. Get on the floor and sit in a comfortable position. Start to breathe deeply. Think hope on the inhale, and heavy on the exhale. Feel that heaviness leave your body as the breath floats upward and outward. Continue that mindful breathing and do a round of single pigeon stretch on both sides. Start by holding for five deep breaths on each leg. Loosening our hip joints is the first tangible step to freeing up creativity and emotion within us. It only takes a few minutes…and it will get your day back on track.

September 29

Small Act of Kindness time! In honor of National Coffee Day, let's do something fun for a total stranger. Go buy two pumpkin spice lattes—one for you of course!—and one for that stranger you see on your travels today. Have you honestly yet to meet someone who doesn't like a pumpkin spice latte? Tiny pebbles create big ripples, Mama. Spread some light—and caffeine—today.

September 30

It is National Mulled Cider Day. And October's Eve. Yes, please...

Mulled Cider Recipe (Food Network)
1 Gallon Apple Cider
½ Cup Brown Sugar
2 tsp Allspice
3 tsp Whole Cloves
4 Cinnamon Sticks
2 Dashes Nutmeg
1 Orange thinly sliced
Rum (Optional)

Combine all the ingredients and simmer in a slow cooker or soup pan for 2 hours. Ladle into cups with a slotted spoon. Add in the rum, if desired, and serve with a long cinnamon stick!

OCTOBER

Make Your Own Magic

October 1

"Delicious Autumn! My very soul is wedded to it, and if I was a bird I would fly about the Earth seeking successive Autumns!" ~George Eliot

Bake some cookies today to celebrate one of the best months of the year! It is National Homemade Cookie Day after all.

October 2

It's October. The month for all kinds of tricks and treats. A time for costumes and clever facades. Embrace your duality, Mama. It's attractive and intriguing…

"I believe in kindness. Also in mischief." ~Mary Oliver, Pulitzer Prize Winner and Poet

…Mischief Managed, indeed.

October 3

My favorite thing about fall is the smells. Look around you. 'Tis the season for sunburnt leaves and cheerful pumpkins. The change in the weather brings a clean crispness that cleanses the earth, and the smoky warmth from fireplace, harvest, and hearth is inviting and peaceful. Fill your home with these intoxicating smells. It's so simple and so fun.

Simmering Fall on the Stove
Fill a small pot with water, orange peels, a few cinnamon sticks, and a handful of whole cloves. Bring to a rolling boil and then back off to a simmer. Let the fragrant steam fill all the nooks and crannies of your home and your heart this autumn.

October 4

"But all the magic I have known I've had to make myself." ~Shel Silverstein

This quote is a gentle and needed reminder at times. We cannot sit back and wait for life to happen to us. For the passion and the interesting and the adventure. We must go seek it, be open to it, and make it ourselves if need be. When you feel stuck or in a rut or frustrated with the monotony that comes at this stage in life, come back to this quote. Come back to yourself. And go find the magic.

October 5

As you bring your body and soul awake this morning say a prayer for yourself. Say a prayer to start this day and your mind on the path that *you need*—not what the outside world pressures you to need. Listen to the silence that only dawn can bring and search your heart for the words…

Place in my heart the courage of a warrior.
Fill my soul with the hope of a sunrise.
Overflow my cup with the love of a mother.

What are you yearning for today?

October 6

Sometimes you just need a little you time. Even an hour away from the mess and chaos and constant disciplining can make all the difference between a stressed out mom and a joyful one. Some mamas have lots of help—but if you don't? You cannot be afraid to reach out and get some. Any way you can. One hour to do something for yourself…work out, take a walk, go shopping, roam Target without a chatty and busy toddler—this is bliss, Mama. This is essential. Don't ever feel guilty for knowing the quiet pleasure that taking care of yourself brings.

October 7

No one can prepare you for the challenges that motherhood brings. The endless patience and the endless repetition is something you just have to experience in order to truly appreciate it. I find myself full of respect and admiration for my mom these days—does this happen to you? It is so honest to God true though what they say...

The days are long but the years are short...

How do we make the most of these long days, Mama? Stay mindful with your family. Stay mindful with yourself. Make time for being alone and with friends. Carve out the life that works for you. Brings you joy. And makes the long days savory and sweet.

October 8

Orange, yellow, red, gold...vibrant and rich. Dancing all around me. Crisp. Cool. I can feel magic just on the edges of the breeze...this is autumn. This is fall. This is the beginning of the most wonderful time of the year. I intend to fully embrace it

October 9

Do you know how special you are, Mama? How strong and soft, inspiring and motivational—how funny and comforting you are? You are all these things, and your whole family knows it. You are a complex and brilliantly capable woman who is a million different things to so many different people. What a humble and powerful and magical place to be.

"Most people think this world we live in is mundane, but you remind us that it's magical. You wrap reality in the wonder and joy of fiction, until it infuses us and becomes true...You're one of life's magicians. You simply haven't realized it yet."
~Menna van Praag, <u>The Dress Shop of Dreams</u>

October 10

Morning Mantra
Sit in a cross-legged position on the floor. Ground yourself with palms flat on your knees and start to deepen the breath. Then start to lift your hands above your head on the inhale, and slowly lower them into prayer in front of your heart on the exhale. Repeat this movement as you begin your affirmation. Think *I am inspiring* as you raise your hands and breathe in. Think *I am successful* as you lower and breathe out. Continue this for as many minutes as you can. Observe how you can lose yourself in the breath and motivation. Invite inspiration in and radiate success out. Believe in that. Believe in yourself.

October 11

*"There is no passion to be found playing small, in settling for a life that is less than the one you are capable of living." ~*Nelson Mandela

Our lives have obligations. Our lives have responsibilities. You may feel stuffed into the Mama box a lot right now—kids are young, they need us so very much at this time in their lives. But this box is not the only thing that defines us. It's a huge, impressive, wonderful box—but it's not the only one. What other box do you dip into these days?

I am an artist
I am a chef
I am a writer
I am a communicator
I am a soul searcher
I am a business owner
I am a creative woman
And yes...I am a Mother.

October 12

"I'm going to make everything around me beautiful. That will be my life."
~Elsie de Wolfe, American Actress, Interior Designer, Author

Elsie de Wolfe lived from 1859-1950. The New Yorker stated that "interior design as a profession was invented" by her, and she spent her life between New York, London, and Paris. She started out as an actress and quickly became enamored with the sets and colors of the stage—which led to her next passion and career as an Interior Decorator. She traded in the browns and beiges that were acceptable in the times for plums and turquoises. She wore what "suited her, regardless of fashion." At the age of 70 she said her morning regimen always consisted of yoga. She had pillows embroidered with the phrase *"Never complain, Never explain."* She wrote books. Let Elsie guide your passion barometer today. In a time when women were fighting for all kinds of rights and lifestyles, this woman followed her inspiration and let dreams come and become reality. (Wikipedia.com)

October 13

A spooky day, a spooky number—is it cold and crisp where you are yet? I feel the pull of my cozy house, Hocus Pocus, and a cup of apple cider. To-do lists can wait; if making memories with your babies is what you want to do—don't hesitate. A surprise movie day will be remembered far longer than dishes and laundry and a clean house.

"Come little children, I'll take thee away
Into the land of enchantment.
Come little children, the time's come to play
Here in my garden of magic."
~Hocus Pocus

October 14

"Life starts all over again when it gets crisp in the Fall." ~F. Scott Fitzgerald

I love this quote as I am a sucker for all things that remind me that we can always start over. Dream new dreams. This year is not yet done with us, and there is still time to make a mark. We inevitably think about the end of the year with the holidays coming on, but there is still time, Mama. Every single day is a day to start over. To live the life that you picture in your head. To be the mom, the wife, the woman that you have always known you can be. Go be that girl...today is as perfect a day as any to start.

October 15

Being a parent is so dual sided. We want our kids to reach for the stars and be independent, passionate adventure seekers, while desperately trying to protect them from all the hurt, disappointment, and dangers in the world. Every day is a mindful study in boundaries—how far do we let our children roam before we lovingly pull them back in? I just want to be a mom who has instilled enough self respect and confidence in her babes that they can handle what life is going to throw at them. And still love the quirks and traits that make them so incredibly unique and amazing. And it all starts now. As young as your little ones are...this mindful parenting starts now.

"Watch carefully the magic that occurs, when you give a person just enough comfort, to be themselves." ~Atticus Finch, Harper Lee, <u>To Kill A Mockingbird</u>

October 16

I have been reading a lot about what it means to be a leader in our communities these days. A leader. Someone that people follow, look up to, respect. A leader gives advice, builds others up, encourages them. A leader must also lead by example—living their life in a way that forces others to notice and be inspired. And no matter what, even in the darkest and hardest of times, leaders just keep going. I needed to hear this today. Even if you don't have all the answers, or you can't see what's waiting around the next turn of events. Persevere. Just keep going. Leaders never quit.

Shall I just insert the word mother in place of leader now or what? Seriously though—we are all leaders. And we became a leader the moment we brought a life into the world, regardless of who or what we were before. So. What kind of leader do you want to be? Who inspired you as a child? Be a leader, Mama. You have no choice, really, so at least be a mindful one...

October 17

I still love the sound of the dawn. It feels like it belongs to the dreamer because the filter of daytime and routine has not affected it yet. Wherever you are, you can hear the birds sing to one another. You can hear your home settling around you. You can hear the air— it passes over buildings and trees and cars and mountains—and it has a sound. Almost like the ocean if you close your eyes. I love the sound of dawn. Join me today in noticing and listening and receiving—and let this short time fill our cups to the brim, so we can pour out that enchantment into others today.

October 18

Do you ever find yourself impatient? Waiting on a call, or a life change, or an event to arrive. Just waiting. And it seems that the world is not on your timetable but on its own. Which can be maddening and disheartening and very, very frustrating.

"When I wait, You strengthen my heart." ~Psalm 27:14

It's hard to let go and accept that not everything will happen right when you want it to. But we have to trust in the process of waiting. It strengthens. It readies.

"There is purpose in your season of waiting." ~Megan Smalley

It will all make sense in the end.

October 19

"Of course size matters. Nobody wants a small glass of wine." ~@rebelcircus

Some days are those days. You know what we're talking about. The wheels came off the wagon, the train is off the tracks, total chaos has ensued. It's ok. Take a deep breath and open the wine fridge.

"I save my carbs for wine. It's called priorities." ~Carrie Bradshaw

October 20

I was reminded by another mom friend today something that truly resonated with me. No matter what has or is or is about to happen in our lives, remember that we chose this life. We chose this husband. We chose to make a family. We chose motherhood. So when you feel yourself frustrated or confused or cranky—gently remind yourself that you chose it. It's a persistent reminder of the gifts God has given us. Choice is a powerful action. It's freedom. And that knowledge can help you take on a difficult day with grace and strength.

Choose: to select from a number of possibilities; pick by preference. To prefer or decide (to do something). To want; desire. (Dictionary.com)

October 21

Mornings have a tendency to start off in a multitude of ways. Sometimes the road blocks a morning throws at you can seem as high as a steaming stack of flapjacks—just not nearly as sweet. Don't let those first few minutes of a long day trap you in a box, Mama. Search out the joy and the funny and the silver linings in these mornings. Don't give up until you find them. Turn on your favorite Pandora station (yes, even if it's a holiday one and it's only October!), stop for a steaming cappuccino at your favorite coffee shop, do 15 minutes of yoga, take a walk. Don't give in to negativity! A great day is waiting—you just have to be determined to *never* settle for less.

"And if you look for (joy) as for silver and search for it as for hidden treasure."
~Proverbs 2:4

October 22

It is National Color Day today. What color are you drawn to this morning? Do you need to attract peace and calm into your day with a subtle blue? Perhaps you need to surround yourself with red to encourage your passions and determination. It is October after all—so maybe you want to bring joy, creativity, and sheer enthusiasm to your world today with Orange. Take a moment to ask yourself—your soul—what it needs on this 22nd day of October.

October 23

Celebrate the small victories. Don't get too caught up in the ultimate endgame that you forget to smile and do a happy dance when something goes right. We have become so weary of taking the compliment or feeling good about our successes. I want my kids—and my husband!—to know when they have done a great job. I want to celebrate the small things. It is too easy to focus on the negative and the criticism in our lives. When was the last time you said, *"I'm proud of you"* or *"you are such a fantastic father"*? Don't wait. Life is too short to let the bad times outweigh the good.

October 24

The dawn brought thoughts of the circle of life today. Perhaps the leaves falling and the new year coming makes me think of endings and beginnings. I know watching my toddler grow up so fast reminds me of how quickly life passes. The definition of the circle of life is this:

Nature's way of taking and giving back life to earth. It symbolizes the universe being sacred and divine. It represents the infinite nature of energy, meaning if something dies it gives new life to another. (Google.com)

Giving back life to earth…so it can give life to another. Change, endings, goodbyes—are all a part of the process. To make way for the next journey.

October 25

"We should spend half of our day simply existing—taking long meals with loved ones, walking, relaxing, and connecting. The BEING is where the self-love and deep gratitude lives. The BEING is where the empowerment is. The BEING is where worth is cultivated. The BEING is where we hear our intuition."
~Jill Willard, Medium and Author of Intuitive Being

This has got to be one of the hardest challenges that comes with motherhood. The BEING. The invitation and allowing of putting the schedule down and just existing with our loved ones. It should come easier than we might think though—motherhood also opens up and expands our sense of intuition. And our intuition is heightened when we give ourselves the permission to simply be. If we want to grow as women, we have to be okay with slowing down first.

October 26

Perspective: *a particular attitude toward or way of regarding something; a point of view (Google.com)*

Sometimes we just need to slow down and consciously ask for some perspective in our day to day lives. It is so easy to let the negative stuff take over our attitudes and ruin the fragile balance of our world. But take a step back, and force yourself to get out of your head for a minute. Find some gratitude for the state that you're in; it will help. You don't have to look far to see the challenges that our brothers and sisters are facing. Perspective. It can change your day from being all about you to being all about how you can help a friend in need.

October 27

Being a mother means being a leader. It means raising the future leaders in our world. So many times I find myself waiting around for something to validate this leadership status—we all do. Fame, fortune, a raise, a promotion, enough Instagram followers—if we just reached a certain level, then we'd really be able and ready to lead others effectively. But this is just not true. We can lead right now. Wherever we are in life. If we think deep instead of wide, we can truly start to make a difference. There are incredible opportunities for leadership all around us every day. The world is just waiting for us to take the first step in showing how powerful and effective we can be.

October 28

"I will see the world today the way that I want my baby to see the world."
~Stephanie Snyder, Yoga Teacher

Start your morning off with an affirmation. The golden rule always works, but this time focus on how you want to see this day. We all want our children to experience a world that is generous, fascinating, and kind. Is that how you see the world?

October 29

Need a last minute Halloween costume? Wrap yourself in tinfoil and go as a leftover. Trust us—it's funny.

And go carve those pumpkins, if you haven't done so yet. It's such a fun tradition to start with your kids...your Annual Family Pumpkin Carving Party!

October 30

All Hallow's Eve. Are you in a spooky mood yet? Ghosts and goblins, princesses and superheroes. October is one of the best months of the year...Let's embrace its magic!

"Listen! The wind is rising and the air is wild with leaves. We've had our summer evenings, now for October eves!" ~Humbert Wolfe, Poet

October 31

Halloween began as a Celtic festival called Samhain. It's said to be the day where the realm between the spirit world and our world was thin—all the fairies and ghosts of the dead could roam free upon the Earth. So the Irish dressed up in costume—so as not to be noticed by all the ghosts—and left out treats on their doorstep to make the spirits happy.

Today it is a day to bring magic and fun to our children's lives. So many wonderful memories come from this day. What traditions can you and your family start this year? It will bring laughter and warmth to those little souls for years and years to come.

NOVEMBER

A Grateful Heart

The Daily Soul Sessions For Every Mama

November 1

The Halloween candy hangover is real y'all. And I'm so grateful for it. Seeing the magic of a holiday through the eyes of our kids brings all the newness and anticipation to life again. It is just the most wonderful time of the year right now. Nothing but holidays, family, friends, music, lights, and deliciousness awaits us.

I am grateful for the feeling of anticipation today.
I am grateful that I get to guide my kids in this time of fairy tales and traditions.
I am grateful for chocolate peanut butter pumpkins.
I am grateful for November.

What are you grateful for today?

November 2

This month is all about settling in and preparing for the winter to come. Even if you live in a sunny climate, November encourages us to surround ourselves with the cozy, the comforting, the sustaining. Our mornings and evenings bring darkness and moonlight. It's a month to cuddle your loved ones and look forward to game nights, crackling fires, hot chocolate, and savory soups. Go ahead and plan that game night with some couple friends this month...fellowship, wine, good food, and great company are all November—and you—need to glow.

November 3

Time. Every day seems to focus on time lately. Too much time, not enough time, wishing time to slow down, waiting for time to pass until bedtime arrives. I don't want us to waste our days waiting for or wanting time to pass. We need to continue to find a way to be content with whatever form time wants to take in our lives. This morning, before the clock really starts to tick away on you, breathe and invite the seconds to pass as they will. Invite your heart and brain to seek out contentment with this day. It might not all go as you hoped or planned—and that is ok. As long as we keep breathing…and thanking God for the time He has given us.

November 4

As this morning dawns, as you lift your head off the pillow, as you hold your first cup of steaming coffee in your hand—find gratitude. Find thankfulness in the breath that travels in and out of your body. Feel joy in the hope that every single sunrise brings. See fascination in the possibilities and adventures yet to unfold. Every single day is another first experience in your life. You've never lived this day before. The first moment with your kids today. The goodbye kiss to your husband. The thousand little decisions and feelings that will pass through you in the next 24 hours. Make them count.

November 5

"To thrive in life you need three bones. A wishbone. A backbone. And a funnybone." ~Reba McEntire

Ahhh to dream, to persevere, to laugh. Country music says a good song tells a great story. And all you need is three chords and the truth. Three things. Any challenge we face—we can face with one of these three things. And that's all we need.

November 6

Do something for yourself today. Just for you. Hit up a yoga class, meet a girlfriend for a quick drink, play that piano for 30 minutes, get outside and take some photos of this gorgeous time of year. The possibilities for creative outlet are endless and endlessly rejuvenating and rewarding for your soul and sanity. Fill your cup so you can fill others'. It's that simple. Make the effort, shrug off the mom guilt, and figure out a little childcare for a short time. Go take care of yourself...calm the storm...soothe your soul...

November 7

Mamas, let's work on our thanksgiving this month. Spite, jealousy, dissatisfaction breeds the same, and I don't want to teach my children that cynical way of life. Rejoice in every sunrise. Laugh at roadblocks. Smile at your neighbors. Do good work and be a good friend. That's it. That's life. Be thankful in every beautiful moment of it today.

"We waste so many days waiting for the weekend. So many nights wanting morning. Our lust for future comfort is the biggest thief of life." ~Joshua Glenn Clark, American Writer

November 8

Accept this day for what it is. Being a mindful mama means a constant practice of finding peace, pleasure, and purpose in each and every moment. We have to learn to find the appreciation in the dark days and thanksgiving in the light. And that comes down to you. Your individual choices and attitude that you have for this world. Sleepless night? Get work done—take that unexpected time to work on your vision board or goal setting. Light some candles for a loved one that needs some extra support. Take your troubles to your yoga mat, pray, read a book that's been calling your name. The more we practice staying mindful and finding the appreciation…the more we will simply begin to appreciate.

November 9

The sun will come up. And light defeats the dark. Every time.

"When the world appears to be most insane, we can't go inside and hide and let the jackals eat up the orchards. We have to respond as humans, which is to say with kindness and wit and caring. We do not—ever—give up. So pull yourself together and get back to work. " ~Tennessee Williams

November 10

What are they saying? Something like six weeks till Christmas. Our neighborhood stores begin to put up their pretty lights, their festive greenery. You begin to think about holiday shopping, you begin to think about next year. Resolutions. What you'll do differently so you aren't in the same spot next November 10th. But it's not too late. It really isn't. Start daily resolutions, not yearly. Let's do something good and positive every day until Thanksgiving. That's at least two weeks of moving in the right direction. Let's. Start. Today.

November 11

As the days get darker and winter can be felt out on the horizon, we consciously seek out the things that comfort, soothe, and take care of us. It is our modern way of preparing for the winter—the storing of foods, packing on insulation for the cold, getting ready for a hibernation, if you will. We are drawn to the known, and taking risks or putting ourselves out there for new ideas is less desirable. This is okay for a little while, if it is what your soul is asking of you. Coming "home", comfort, and working on your insulation can only better prepare you for when you feel like going out on a limb again.

November 12

Sometimes the small acts of kindness we show the world stick with our children more deeply than the big stuff we want to impress upon them every day. This holiday season there are so many small acts of kindness we can involve ourselves and families in! Grab some gallon Ziploc bags and head to the dollar store. Fill the bags with a toothbrush, toothpaste, hand sanitizer, protein bars, a small bottle of water—any small daily necessities you can find. Add a handwritten note of inspiration. These blessing bags are wonderful to keep in your car and hand out to the homeless. Small acts of kindness make a huge impact in the world.

November 13

"Some days I'm confident. Some days I feel like a loser. There are no successful people who never feel like losers. They don't exist." ~Diane von Furstenberg

Let's find the same faith during the lows as we do during the highs today.

November 14

Are you facing any storms these days? Whether you're picking up the pieces of debris from the aftermath or still watching the clouds loom in the distance, the stressful times in our lives are the times when all this work on staying mindful, staying thankful, staying centered come into play. The practice of letting go, thanking God, and finding joy and true creativity in the small moments is the practice that will keep our hearts unblocked when the ship is tossed about in rough waters. We can stay steady, Mama. And that fearless pursuit of right and unwillingness to break becomes inspiration—becomes a beacon of light for your community around you.

November 15

Pick up your pen today and journal. Grab an adult coloring book. Maybe it's pulling out your camera and capturing some magic today. Whatever creative outlet you choose, focus on gratitude. Think about the small gifts you've been given in this stage of your life and honor them. November is the month for Thanksgiving—for remembering all the truly miraculous blessings we have received. It is not the time to stay silent about them, but rather put that gratitude out in the world. There is nothing more powerful or transformative to yourself and those around you than a grateful heart.

"Gratitude turns what we have into enough, and more. It turns denial into acceptance, chaos into order, confusion into clarity...it makes sense of our past, brings peace for today, and creates a vision for tomorrow." ~Melody Beattie, Author

November 16

There is simply no room for pity, disappointment, jealousy, or dissatisfaction in the midst of gratitude. Remember that when you feel the depression or disenchantment sneak in. This one tool, this one weapon, this one simple act of gratitude is all we need to find the light. This is what we have to teach our children. So they too can seek out the light.

"Lord may my child have a grateful heart." ~Hebrews 13:15

November 17

I came across an interesting thought today that I wanted to share.

Respond
Over
React

I kind of love this as we navigate these choppy parenthood years. It is so easy to simply react to our children, our society, our day. And reaction can be emotional and knee jerk—and tend to end in yelling or anger. Instead, I want to work on responding to the things this world sets in my path. To take a moment to think, pray, reflect before words leave my lips or actions stir my body. To be a woman who isn't tossed immediately in the wind—but is steadfast and wise. That is what is inspiring me today.

November 18

"Honor the space between no longer and not yet." ~Nancy Levin, Author

Sometimes the burning to be "someone" becomes exhausting. We all want to leave a legacy, do great things, be remembered for our accomplishments. And you constantly feel like getting there is taking too much time. But that space between the past and the future? That is right now. That is today. And what you do today is all that really matters. Forgive yourself, let yourself off the hook for one moment and just work on being the best mom, the best friend you can be today. Read that book to your kids, take that friend out for a happy hour drink. Connect. That is all the legacy that really matters. Today.

November 19

"When you arise in the morning, think of what a precious privilege it is to be alive—to breathe, to think, to enjoy, to love." ~Marcus Aurelius

Infuse your day with these thoughts. These simple privileges that we are blessed to be able to do. How do we teach ourselves and our families to not take this for granted? I think the first step is to speak your gratitude out loud. At the dinner table, in the car on the way to run errands, in bed at night with your love—share what you are grateful for. Especially the small things—the things we do take for granted that so many are struggling without. And the next step? Give back. Get involved somehow and give back. Tis a blessing to receive. Tis a bigger blessing to give.

November 20

"When nothing is sure, everything is possible." ~Margaret Drabble, Author

Times of change are so powerful. There is so much hope and opportunity and possibility if we can just focus on that part of the puzzle. Not the fear. The fear will paralyze you and stall your heart, soul, and dreams. But we were made for awesome things, Mama. And we cannot be afraid of change. So run after that uncertainty like we run after a glass of wine at 5—er 4:30—pm. Because anything...and I mean anything...is possible in this world.

November 21

Sometimes life takes us into a season—however long or short—of challenge. Holidays can be one such season to some of us. Travel, family, loss, in-laws, healthy habits—I can see these challenges before they even arrive. So today I am making Thanksgiving my mantra. All day long. All week long. All month long if I have to. I will answer stress with affirmations of joy and gratitude. I will try to find the humor in certain situations, and I will take the potential negatives of getting out of routine with grace and lots and lots of breathing. Stay mindful this week. It takes practice…and it's possible.

November 22

Do you ever take a moment to just be? Do you ever step outside into the cool darkness of night and glance up at the stars? Have you ever walked alone on a beach, sat in the sand and observed the waves crashing over and over? Or put on your favorite song, closed your eyes and let the music wash into you, over you, through you. Our worlds are so messy, chaotic, and loud these days—and thank God for it. But it is hard to hear your own heart, your own truth through all this noise.

Find a moment today to be by yourself—not easy, I know. But it is incredibly important to mindfully observe something much, much bigger than the world we inhabit on a daily basis. This practice is healing. And inspiring. And powerful.

November 23

"Sometimes the smallest things take up the most room in your heart." ~Winnie the Pooh

I am filled with humility and gratitude at the blessings in my life. Each beautiful face that I get to see today is a gift God graces me with. I stand in awe that such love exists and that I get the chance to experience it.

Positive Affirmations. Let them fill your heart with that joyful feeling. Allow that joy to seep into every bone and vessel of yourself. That's when you know they are working.

November 24

Life is all about attracting the good in our lives and keeping out the bad. That is the prayer we say with our baby girl every night. Bring in the good, keep out the bad. While we can't keep out all the bad, we can certainly create positive thoughts and habits and actions that can only make space for the interesting and enlightening things in this world. If we let negativity and stress win out, it will eat us alive. We know this. It's a spiral that can quickly become overpowering. So choose positivity and grace instead. What could it possibly hurt anyway?

"A grateful heart is a magnet for miracles." ~Unknown

November 25

There is something truly mystical about this time of year. It must be the traditions, the family, the sense of homecoming that these special holidays bring. Memories from your childhood mix with the new memories you're creating. They swirl together in sparkle and light for your children...for yourself. If we can get past the stress and strain that this time of year uncovers, and tap into the wonder and magic of it—our hearts can rest light and free. We can soak in all the peace and promise that's waiting. And the secret to letting go of that stress is to stay in the moment. Stay mindful. Stay grateful. Stay forgiving.

Journal about a favorite childhood holiday tradition. Bring to life that tradition in your own family this season. These repeated times of love and light left an impact on you...so our job is to do the same for the next generation.

November 26

A foggy dawn has me shivering for a thick sweater and a hot cup of coffee. A fire, some holiday music in the air, and my favorite journal all set me up for a lovely morning of dreaming, scheming, and goal setting for the coming weeks. I dare you to try this am ritual once a week. Before the iPhone gets switched on, before Instagram and Facebook are scrolled, before you let the world into your world, take the time to surround yourself with comfort and home. Soulfully consider what you want to bring into your life and accomplish, experience, or teach in the coming days. Sometimes goals can be big brilliant things that loom in the distance...and sometimes they can be glowing embers that you snatch out of the air and make a part of your life today.

November 27

Where does this deep November day find you, Mama? Are you at home? Out of town? With lots of people and friends, or perhaps just your sweet little family. Has Thanksgiving come and gone or are you still busily preparing for it? Wherever this day finds you—stop. Slow down and be present in the moment. Don't rush to the next meal, the next minute, the next plane ride. Just stop. Enjoy the people surrounding you, listen to their stories, share your own. Don't worry about the germs those little ones are passing back and forth—instead rejoice in how sweetly they play together. Smile and secretly cheers your mother or mother-in-law when the "advice" starts flowing. The foggy mamahood years can cause us to blur the time away—but try pushing through the haze to find the absolute magic all around you.

"The real gift of gratitude is the more grateful you are, the more present you become." ~Robert Holden

November 28

"The struggle ends when gratitude begins." ~Neale Donald Walsch

Every single person on this Earth has their own unique challenges today. Our first mistake as caregivers and inspiration igniters is to forget that in our day to day encounters. From the struggle of a strong willed toddler, to a marital fight, to a loss of a loved one— soften your heart to this world. Listen to the silence in between conversation. Look for the positive glimmers in a complicated situation. Start your every breath with gratitude. Immediately going on the offensive can be so second nature to us mama bears...so let's be peacemakers above all instead.

If you need some guidance in this peacemaking department, try yoga. The mix of spiritual and physical is the perfect cocktail for letting go, letting in, and letting be.

November 29

Discipline. Willpower. Determination. Making the decision to do something is the easy part. But do I have the discipline to see it through? To keep going when the going gets hard. To keep finding inspiration when yet another roadblock is thrown up in my path. I want to say yes. But deep down I know it takes a lot of preparation to set yourself up for success. You need coaches, you need dream boards, you need THE reason *why* you are reaching for whatever goals you've set for yourself.

For right now though, I just want to hold on to that really special moment when I decide I'm going to do something new. It's a powerful feeling—full of motivation and magic. If I can bottle this feeling up, maybe I can come back to it in those silly moments of doubt or frustration. Light beats the dark. And I really like the light.

"You've always had the power, my dear. You just had to learn it for yourself."
~Glinda the Good Witch, The Wizard of Oz

November 30

Dawn greets you with the whisper of *tradition* in the air. What does that word mean to you? Do you come from a childhood rich with tradition? Or are you creating your own as you raise your family? Even if you had tons of traditions growing up—things change, life happens. I find myself struggling to hold onto or perfectly recreate some of the traditions I had as a little girl. But it just doesn't work that way. Hopefully I can continue most of the special memories, but I have to be open to new magic as well. I have a husband with his own ideas of what tradition is, for one. I think the point of tradition is to start it while your babies are young—so they can experience the wonder and sparkle and joy that this time of year brings.

DECEMBER

Believe in Miracles

The Daily Soul Sessions For Every Mama

December 1

Miracles float in the air this month like snowflakes in a soft storm. Close your eyes, lift your face to the heavens, and smell the sharp promise of a coming flurry. We spend so much time dreaming and setting goals and making life happen—we can forget how to stop and just let life happen. This world has delights and adventures in store for you that you couldn't possibly come up with in your wildest dreams. How exciting is that? Today I want to make room for the possibilities I've yet to ponder...the unimaginable, if you will. It's all about staying open, staying present, staying free.

"Keep some room in your heart for the unimaginable." ~Mary Oliver, Poet

December 2

The word waiting has been in the atmosphere lately. We are all waiting on something...so what are you waiting for, Mama? A child to sleep? A marriage to heal? A baby to come? A phone call to bring some news? The holidays to arrive to see loved ones? Whatever it is, we all have prayers that have yet to be answered, and that can be a hard season to find mindfulness and contentment in. To wait is to be in some form of suspension or unsettlement...it is so hard to have to postpone the very outcome your soul desires. And yet. And yet. And yet...our lives are filled with waiting. So we must fill those periods with peace, acceptance, and the unshakeable knowledge that there is always hope—this season is brimming over with hope. As long as we wait, there is always hope.

December 3

A gift that we want. A gift that we need. A gift that we'll wear. A gift that we'll read. I truly love this guide to gift buying as the holidays come.

"Maybe Christmas doesn't come from a store. Maybe Christmas, perhaps means a little bit more!" ~The Grinch, How the Grinch Stole Christmas by Dr. Seuss

December 4

This month is an earth element month. We bring trees and greenery inside, light fires, and prepare for the winter season ahead. We spend time in the kitchen, baking, thinking about ways to bring cheer to our loved ones. We are also on the go at parties non-stop, which can contradict that earth element and wear you out. It's a busy month— not a whole lot of time for personal dream following, so we must steal whatever moments of solitude we can. And revel in the creativity that gift giving, kitchen magic, and spending time with loved ones brings. 'Tis the most wonderful time of the year after all.

December 5

There are a handful of days left in this year. Don't wait one more second to make some dreams come true. December is the month for joy, peace, and to finish what we've started. Come on, Mama, what have you started that needs some completion? We all know the satisfaction that comes from a successfully finished project, naptime, or potty training session. So let's chase that satisfaction! Let's finish what we've started.

December 6

Find the humor in this day. Whatever you are facing—face it with a smile. Respond with love. With laughter. With a light heart. Be stubborn in your refusal to go to the dark side. Use light sabers, sweet smelling candles, dance parties, red wine—WHATEVER—at your disposal to find the light. Life is so much sweeter when we do.

December 7

Twinkle lights and a crackling fire make inspiration easy to find. An early morning, coffee, and my journal—my essentials this season to maintaining balance and peace. The key word being peace. What is it about the holidays that wire our children up like a wind-up toy? I want to capture that anticipation and magic in their eyes and carry it with me wherever I go, all year long. However everything must balance the other out, right? Especially after we turn—eh hem—older. So what brings you a moment of calm, Mama? Ten minutes of meditation? A sketch book? A daily photography prompt? We have to continually remind ourselves to seek out those moments of creativity—and it is never more essential than right now.

December 8

"If you believe it will work out, you'll see opportunities. If you believe it won't, you will see obstacles." ~Wayne Dyer

I think I can. I think I can…I know I can. I know I can. Now is the time for miracles, for magic. For believing in yourself and your kids and your husband. Every single time we choose optimism over pessimism—change over fear—great things happen. Small slices of light break through our rigid outlook and inspiration follows. I know we can, Mama. Do you believe it?

December 9

This month is the time for hope and believing. The fifth chakra, the heart chakra, represents those elements. Bring more magic of the season into your life today with a little focus on that heart chakra. Surround yourself with the color green, love others, make an outward show of affection for the people in your life. Make an outward show of affection toward yourself as well. Diffuse lavender, rose or lemon essential oil if you have it, and use these affirmations today:

I am loved.
My life is balanced and peaceful.
I feel grace and gratitude in everyone I encounter.

December 10

Open your heart to the magic of the holidays. They can bring surprising and new traditions into our lives. Our tribe of friends and family have recently started a Holiday Home Tour—basically a fantastic way for all of us to see some of our friends' delightfully decorated homes that we otherwise wouldn't see this season. Keep it simple, keep it fun—keep it at three to four houses and stay at each home for only 45 minutes to an hour. The first home had wine and apps and pizza for the kiddos. The second home had pin the tail on Rudolph and more wine (obviously!). The last house had dessert and a cookie decorating station for the kids! Followed up by the movie Elf in the living room for the enchanted and exhausted toddlers, while the adults chatted and found the Holiday Spirit in the lights, the friendship, the food, and the fun. Tradition. Check, check, and check!

December 11

20 days. 20 days til the clock starts over, the calendar flips new, the Earth grows one year older. A lot can happen in 20 days—new habits established, old habits banished. Never stop dreaming, Mama…some of us work best under pressure.

"In the end, we only regret the chances we didn't take." ~Lewis Carroll

December 12

Rest. Relax. Enjoy. Peace. Breathe. Illuminate. Remember. Create. Let these words flow through your morning as the light filters in your kitchen window. The latest lesson to learn in motherhood is to not push yourself too hard this season. Recognize when you've had your kids up too late, had yourself up too late, been to too many festivities, and plain tuckered yourselves out. It is ok to say no sometimes. It's ok to stay at home and drink hot chocolate and make art with your kids for Christmas cards, and just create memories. With your feet up on the couch, preferably. Relaxation is a gift that we must seek out, will into existence, and then accept it graciously and warmly when it arrives.

December 13

Faith: complete trust or confidence in someone or something. (Google.com)

December is a sweet reminder of how to encourage faith in a day to day existence. Santa, Elf on the Shelf, traditions, lighting a menorah, time with family, candy canes (if you're my kid)—and up to the birth of Jesus, the North Star, the Son of God—December is brimming with things to be faithful in. And let's add one more. Let's have faith in ourselves. Let's have complete trust and confidence in what amazing women we are. What life changing mamas we have worked to be this year. Faith in ourselves can shape the world, one sweet day at a time. Faith is the first step—the foundation—in every adventure we take.

December 14

"Spring passes and one remembers one's innocence.
Summer passes and one remembers one's exuberance.
Autumn passes and one remembers one's reverence.
Winter passes and one remembers one's perseverance."
~Yoko Ono

What a fascinating summary of what a year can bring into our lives. New beginnings and hope. Excitement and passion for life. Respect for all that has come before and the fragility of every day. And how strong we are. How determined. We are all survivors, Mama. It is how we choose to show the world just how we handle this surviving that makes us beautiful and unique.

December 15

"The unexpected is usually what brings the unbelievable." ~Mandy Kellogg
Rye, MKR

Do not be afraid of the unknown in this life. Letting go of our desperate need for control is essential to our self-care and mindful journey. The best surprises and most satisfying days sometimes come from activities and events that we had no idea were in store. I find grounding and peace in that thought when I feel like my world may be spinning a little crazier than I'd like it to. Embrace the unexpected today. The Universe may know just what we need more than we do.

December 16

If anyone is groomed and open to believing in miracles, it is us. The mothers in this world. To know how it feels to create, nurture, and grow a life inside of your body—or to know how it feels to raise a totally unique and unblemished soul—that is what a miracle is. We forget how AWEsome it is to be able to do what we do. We forget that every child is a gift specifically designed for us to take care of. To teach. And to pass on the wonder and hope that miracles bring.

December 17

Bring winter into your home and try diffusing orange, thieves, and cedarwood essential oils. The mix of citrus, clove, and woods will have you reaching for a mug of hot cocoa, a thick pair of socks, your loves, and a feel good holiday movie. Bonus—thieves essential oil is great for the immune system in this germy, staying indoors month!

December 18

"Snow falling soundlessly in the middle of the night will always fill my heart with sweet clarity." ~Novala Takemoto

There is nothing so soothing, so peaceful, so meditative as a gentle snowstorm. Perhaps only the waves crashing on a shore can rival it. But the snow—pure and unique—takes over the sky and transforms our slice of this world into a magical snow globe, with not one flake like the other. Just like us. Our children. Our community. We are all gloriously unique and special, and our purpose this day is to embrace what gifts we alone have been given. Then share them with everyone we can.

December 19

Enjoy these "Holiday Hacks"!

Don't want to do a whole month of Elf on the Shelf? Just do it for the last 10 days!

White wine takes out red wine stains...just sayin'.

Buy a few Water Wow coloring books (available on Amazon) to have on hand for a last minute little one gift.

December 20

"I believe in Pink. I believe that laughing is the best calorie burner. I believe in kissing, kissing a lot. I believe in being strong when everything seems to be going wrong. I believe that happy girls are the prettiest girls. I believe that tomorrow is another day and I believe in miracles." ~Audrey Hepburn

Yassss. Amen. Mic drop. 'Nuff said. Peace out.

December 21

The Winter Solstice. The shortest sunlit day of the year is upon us. Hold your family tight, find gratitude in this amazing planet, this amazing year, and this amazing life that has brought you to this very second. The season for miracles fills every crack and crevice of doubt and fear you may have—let it. And just think, halfway around the world millions of souls are celebrating the exact opposite. Light rules the day there. Light is always around us—you just have to flip the switch, Mama.

December 22

Winter is coming…more like winter has come. Let your inner introvert loose. It's the perfect time to focus inward. Focus on family. Focus on yourself. We all need to recharge our batteries in different ways–and this time of year is perfect for that. Whether you need to close the doors and be alone or find the party and outside stimulation—this month has got it all. You can't pour from an empty cup…so find your way to refill it.

December 23

"Yesterday is history. Tomorrow is a mystery. Today is a gift. That is why we call it The Present." ~A.A. Milne

The season of giving is a great one. We can teach what true giving means to our little ones. To give without expectation. Because what we give we get back in a hundred humbling and fulfilling ways. This day can be quite chaotic if we let it. Or we can go with the flow of its energy—and focus on how we can give. How we can make this world a little bit brighter—a little bit better—for someone we love.

December 24

Anticipation: *Expectation or hope. (Dictionary.com)*

If there is one day of the year that is filled with anticipation by much of this world, today is it. The high expectations of certain gifts, the bona fide pure hope emitting from your child's eyes—'tis a magical day indeed. I thrive on anticipation. We all should. That butterfly feeling of all good things to come is how every single day should be experienced. It really is a study in living in the moment, because whatever is in store for us, we are living with hope for the future right now.

December 25

"True love was born in a stable." ~Unknown

If we can live our lives with love first, then we will live well, Mama. And love is simple. It is humble. It is unassuming. Love is freely given, and it expects nothing in return. Love is beautiful. And we experience it every single day we get to see our children grow. Which makes love a living miracle. And that is freaking awesome.

December 26

"If your actions create a legacy that inspires others to dream more, learn more, do more, and become more, then you are an excellent leader." ~Dolly Parton

Begin to seek out mantras and resolutions to serve you in the coming new year. Open your heart to its desires today, Mama. This quote struck a chord. What legacy do you want to create next?

December 27

This time between the end of the holidays and the beginning of the new year is a powerful one. I can feel winter settling in for a long stay—yet the bubbling current of energy that a brand new year brings is present too. Are you still racing around from one family member to the next? Is your toddler convinced that Christmas must last forever? Try to find some time to hibernate with your family this week. We all need a little taste of home and safety and peace after the whirlwind of the past month. Savory soups, puzzles, movie nights—it's time to truly savor this phase of your life with your family. It is so precious—and challenging—and exhausting—and magical. And we don't want to miss a moment of it.

December 28

This year. This incredible year is coming to a close. We did it. We got through all the sleeping, the not sleeping, the potty training, the food battles, the tantrums, the practices, the homework, the battle of wills. And we got to experience all the giggles, the cuddles, the I love yous, and the pure joy of watching a soul that came from you thrive. How can 365 days feel both long and so very short at the same time? And as challenging as parts—ok pretty much all—of this motherhood journey is…we are still here. Breathing and loving and smiling and kicking booty. Close your eyes for just a moment, and find gratitude in the warrior goddess mother that you are. Be thankful for the creativity you have brought into your life and for each and every goal you set for yourself this year and then totally crushed. The end of a year is a time for celebration—and this party is just getting started.

December 29

Get to your yoga mat, favorite spin class, or gym today. Move the body that has got to be exhausted from a completely fantastic month. Some of us are happy, some of us are struggling, some of us are simply relieved that December is almost over. Whatever category your soul is in, your body will thank you for a little TLC today. In this time before major change, it can be calming and motivating to find some routine, some sweat, and some endorphins within your heart beats.

December 30

Reset: *To set again or differently (Google.com)*

This is it. The end of a 365 day adventure. The best part about endings is the beginnings that are anxiously waiting just around the corner. The best part about endings is that we get to decide how we move forward into this vast and glorious future. What parts of our journey and self discovery do we want to take with us, and what parts do we want to leave behind? It is up to you, Mama. Take some moments today and journal on that. As the time for reset approaches, write down the best and not so best parts of this year. The lessons learned and habits made that are serving you well, and what new challenges you want to take on. There is nothing as exciting as a new beginning...embrace that positive and hopeful energy...and reset.

December 31

Repeat after me: I am grateful for this glorious year. I am grateful for the memories I've made. I am grateful for all the surprises along the way. I am grateful for the time to follow my dreams. I am grateful for the chance to pass on strength and confidence and fearlessness to my children. I am grateful to be a woman. I am grateful to be a mom. I am grateful for one more trip around the sun.

"And now we welcome the New Year, filled with things that have never been."
~Rainer Maria Rilke, Writer

Want more inspiration?

Go to TheDailySoulSessions.com to get your
30 Day Journaling Challenge!
Each day has a new journal prompt that encourages you to dig deep
and open up your creative well. No prompt takes longer than 10
minutes if you don't want it to, so there are no excuses!

Get Your Free Lullaby Download by Leaving a Review on Amazon!

Please help spread the word and the love by leaving a review on
Amazon for <u>The Daily Soul Sessions For Every Mama</u>

After you leave a review, send us a screenshot of your review to
contact@thedailysoulsessions.com and we will send you a free
download of the soothing lullaby "Light" by Kate and Kacey
Coppola! Sweetly rock those babes to sleep...zzzzzz.

About The Daily Soul Sessions

Join our Tribe! We are passionate about making dreams come true.

We are committed to light and love and finding joy in Every. Single. Day.

www.TheDailySoulSessions.com

Instagram
@thedailysoulsessions

Twitter
@dailysoulsesh

Facebook
/thedailysoulsessions

Our Deepest Thanks...

This journey would never have happened without so many people. To our parents, there will never be enough *thank you's* in this world to truly tell you how much your support and generosity over the years means to us. To our husbands—being a mom is by far the craziest adventure we've been on yet, and we wouldn't want to go on it with anyone but you guys. To all of our TDSS tribe out there in this world, we thank you for inspiring us to be the best women, the best moms we can be.

Thank you God for the gift of creativity. We will strive to be worthy of that gift every day.

Salute!

About the Authors

Kacey, Kate, and Kara are sisters and mamas who love to cook, drink Italian wine, make music, and unexpectedly have babies within months of each other. Kate and Kacey are identical twins and Grammy nominated songwriters and recording artists. Kara is a passionate blogger and photographer with experience in PR and marketing for the fine arts. Their first book, The Daily Soul Sessions For The Pregnant Mama is cherished by mamas-to-be all across the world. It's 280 soul sessions, one for every day of pregnancy. Following up that book with this one was only natural—motherhood is no joke!

They love to follow their dreams whether it be writing books, singing on the radio, doing a headstand in yoga class, or finally living in the same city at the same time. They currently reside with their husbands, kids, and dogs in Redondo Beach, California and Denver, Colorado. You can follow their adventures on Instagram: @thedailysoulsessions

70877658R00132

Made in the USA
San Bernardino, CA
09 March 2018